He
Speaks
Softly

BOB BENSON

He Speaks Softly

Learning to Hear God's Voice

Guideposts

CARMEL • NEW YORK 10512

This Guideposts edition is published by
special arrangement with Word, Inc.

HE SPEAKS SOFTLY: LEARNING TO HEAR GOD'S VOICE

Copyright © 1985 by Bob Benson
Printed in the United States of America

Portions of this material originally appeared in *Meanings*.

Library of Congress Cataloging in Publication Data

Benson, Bob.
    He speaks softly.

    Bibliography: p.
    1. Vocation, Ecclesiastical. 2. Christian life—1960–
I. Title.
BV4740.B46   1985   248.8'8   85-3296

To my two eldest sons,
Robert, with the skills and views of a professional
copywriter and advertising man,
and *Michael,* with the talents and concerns of a
pastor and student of the Word.
Readers and writers of words and ideas themselves,
they took time to advise and encourage their father.

Contents

1

He Is a God
Who Speaks

". . . you also are . . . called to belong to Jesus Christ."

*Think of it, all that speech pouring down, selling nothing, judging nobody.
. . . What a thing it is to sit absolutely alone, cherished by this wonderful,
unintelligible, perfectly innocent speech, the most comforting speech in the
world, the talk that rain makes all by itself all over the ridges. . . . Nobody
started it, nobody is going to stop it. It will talk as long as it wants, this
rain. As long as it talks I am going to listen.*

THOMAS MERTON[1]

1
He Is a God
Who Speaks

I'm sure she meant something different.

Her question went deeper than just what we were talking about at the moment. I was familiar with her question. I think I see it all the time on people's faces when I'm speaking. She asked me point-blank, "What is it that you are trying to say?"

The query came at the end of an interview for a radio program. I'm not always as excited about being interviewed as I might be. Maybe it is because I am basically a private person. But partly it is because it always seems to me that the questions are rather mundane and so I end up giving what seems to me mundane answers. Thus neither one of us appears as witty and intelligent as we both undoubtedly must be!

This interviewer was good at her job, though, and I was stimulated both by the perceptiveness of her inquiries and the depth and brilliance of my responses. I was almost disappointed when she indicated that there was only this one final question she wanted to ask before turning off the tape machine. "What is it that you are trying to say?"

I don't think I had ever tried to answer this question in a brief sentence or two. Or even in a paragraph. I must have thought of

11

it before because lurking somewhere in the back of my mind there was an answer. Apparently it had just been waiting for an invitation to come out. Especially for all those folks out in radioland. So out it came. I don't know who was the most surprised when it did, the interviewer or the interviewee. But in just seven concise, well-chosen words I gave my response.

It was a sort of a mission statement for me. Now I would remind you that a mission statement is not as easy to come by as you might imagine. Once I spent the better part of a night with the senior management staff of the family music company trying to put into words how we felt the mission of the business could best be defined. Such a statement, when properly worded and authentic, can help direct a company into future endeavors, as well as help indicate some areas from which time and capital should be withdrawn.

So here I suddenly was with my mission statement expressing the fundamental, underlying truth of all I want to do and to be. I wonder if you, given the challenge, could tell the rest of us the one thing that you would like us to remember about your life?

When I realize now that I can express in as few words as seven the deep foundational truth of my life I wonder what I am doing writing another book. Why don't I just put out a new bumper sticker or get the government to issue a new postage stamp with my message emblazoned on it? When I tell people in the first service of a retreat or conference that I can express all I really need to say to them in a single sentence, I can almost hear them thinking out loud, "Well, why don't you just go ahead and say it and get it over with—and then we can go out and play golf or go shopping?" I usually tease them for a little while but in the end I always tell them.

The truth is, though, when I get ready to say the seven words I always seem to feel the need to digress and first tell everyone what those seven words have come to mean to me and how they have changed my life. Then I get to telling stories I have heard or read about other people who have come to believe the same things—and it takes me awhile to say my seven words. In fact, I can usually use about as much time as the listeners will allow.

Even at the risk of your reading them and putting the book back on the counter, I am going to go ahead and tell you my seven words. Because if you begin to truly believe them, I will have said enough to you anyway. My words are:

God Has Something to Say to You!

Of course, I am hoping that you realize that these seven words are much more profound than they first appear to be. And I am hoping that you will want to discover what else I have to say about them. I do have lots to say and many stories to tell. But all the things I believe begin here. Nothing is more important to me than believing that God is a God who speaks to us. If you will read on then I will tell you how I have come to believe this so strongly.

In my office I have a collection of Bibles and Testaments on the bottom shelf of my bookcase. All of them together, from the Thompson Chain Reference Edition of the King James Version, through the Phillips, the Revised Standard Version, the New English Bible, and the New International Version, mark my sporadic journeys with the Word for nearly forty years. One of the volumes, now tattered with age, is a Precious Promise Testament of the King James Authorized Version with the words of Jesus in red.

I used it in my younger days when I was a new convert and later when I became a student preacher. Until recently, in fact, unless my text was from the Old Testament, I have generally carried a New Testament when I preached. Something happened which made me change my idea about that old habit. I was sitting on the platform with a preacher friend of mine in a conference where we were taking turns speaking. He was a man who obviously loved the Word with a deep intensity. He had a large Bible under his arm and I had my New Testament in my hand. He leaned over to me and said, "I sure do admire all you folk who can memorize the Old Testament and just carry the New one with you." I decided then and there to go out and get myself a whole, big Bible to carry and use from that point on!

My first sermon, however, was preached from that little Precious Promise Testament. In its flyleaf, there is a calendar marking some events that occurred in my teen-age years. Each was an event that had deep significance in my life.

7/15/46   saved *Tennessee District Campmeeting*
8/28/46   sanctified *Ruskin Campmeeting*
8/24/47   called to preach *Ruskin Campmeeting*
8/26/48   first sermon *Ruskin Campmeeting*

Each of those notations marks a time at which I heard God speaking to me. I must confess that on each occasion whatever he said came in such a quiet, gentle way that I did not then, and perhaps still don't, fully understand. I only know that they were turning points for me.

On the evening first noted in mid-July of 1946 I do not recall anything that would have even remotely warned me I was going to round a corner. It would send me in one direction—however fitfully—for the rest of my life. In all likelihood on that summer night in 1946, Gene Williams, Bill Anderson and I went out to the Trevecca campus to the Tennessee District Campmeeting in the absence of something better to do. It may have been that my Dad, who was the song leader for the meeting, had offered to let us take him home after service and use the Dodge afterward if we would go and sing in the choir. He had a little Chinese proverb that he often quoted, to me in particular, "No singee, no ridee." But I am quite sure that I didn't join the crowd in the tent pitched on the basketball court next to old Hardy Hall that night with the express purpose of "getting saved."

To my recollection, I had never gone forward or made any kind of profession of faith previous to that evening. To this day I cannot remember having even thought about it until the invitation was given that night. Gene had "gotten religion" a Sunday night or so before, and when they sang the invitation song, he asked Bill and me if we would like to go to the altar. I remember he said we could all go down together. The three of us went forward that night for prayer.

I don't recall much about kneeling there with the altar workers who alternated between telling the penitents to "let go" and to "hold on." I don't remember what I prayed and I can't tell you any answers that I heard coming back to me either. For that matter, I couldn't tell you precisely what I heard God say to me at any of the other times that are duly noted in my Precious Promise Testament. And it is certain that the outline for that first sermon has been long forgotten by both the speaker and the hearers. But I do know it was on those occasions I first began to recognize the calling voice of God in such a way that I responded and obeyed.

It's probably true that back then my perception of his calling to me was rather strict and precise. It was in terms of a specific vocation and a way of religious life in which I had been brought up. It is only from the perspective of my life now that I am coming to see the words *called* and *calling* in a much broader context: the way Paul most often, uses them in his writings in the New Testament.

The Greek word for *called* is *kaleo*. Paul uses forms of the word over forty times. In only two of those places, Romans 1:1 and 1 Corinthians 1:1, does he use *called* to mean his special, personal commission to be an apostle. Everywhere else in his writings he uses *called* and *calling* to mean a process by which God leads people out of their bondage to this world, so that he may justify and sanctify them and bring them into his service. It is a process which takes place as we hear the gospel, and it brings us into fellowship with Christ. At the same time, it creates the fellowship of the body of believers. Thus Paul addresses church members everywhere as "called ones" and describes us as "called to be saints."

The root word *kaleo* appears in other words that we know and use. It is the word from which we get *exhort*, which means "to summon or to call." *Paraclete*, one of the names for the Holy Spirit, is a compound word derived from *kaleo* and it means "the one who is called alongside to bring us aid." A word we probably are even more familiar with is *ecclesia*, from which we get the word *church*. And it literally means "the called ones."

So it may be unfortunate then, that in present day usage "called of God" has come to mean the special selection of persons for the so-called "full time" ministry. The primary meaning in the writings of Paul is that the calling is for every man. It is important to understand that Paul was addressing all of us when he wrote, ". . . you also are . . . called to belong to Jesus Christ" (Romans 1:6).

The caller is God. The call comes to us from God. The Bible is the story of a God who is constantly calling us and coming to us. This is probably not expressed better anywhere than in Revelation 3:20 when God says, "Behold, I stand at the door and knock: if any man hear my voice and open the door, I will come in to him, and will sup with him, and he with me" (KJV). There is a very deep sense in which our calling on him is not calling at all; it is our belated answer to his gentle, persistent, ever-present calling to us.

I don't believe that God suddenly decided that he would speak to me in the summer of my sixteenth year. Rather, long before that night when I "went forward," in ways I cannot even remember and in processes I could not see or even suspect, he had been standing at the door of my heart and knocking so that I might hear and obey his voice.

I have come to know that those brief encounters in the life of a teenager were only the beginnings of his message to me. Those experiences, as important as they were in the directing of my life, were more like the start of a dialogue. It was not as if he had now told me what I needed to know and then just hung up the phone on me. He was not finished with his call for me, he was just beginning. And he still does not seem to be through telling me what he would have me know and do and be.

Looking back across the nearly forty years that have passed since I first responded to the voice I heard, I am aware of coming to places in my life which I never could have imagined while kneeling there in the straw at Ruskin. His providences and purposes have steadfastly moved and worked in and around the circumstances of my life. My choices and commitments, sometimes faithful and true, sometimes hazy and weak, have also been ways that his words have been relayed to me. Even now his calling to me is being reshaped and refined. It is as fresh and new as the morning.

I have come to be a purveyor of words, a dealer in ideas and phrases. I am a speaker and a writer, a user of words, a bearer of truth. Words are the tools of my chosen craft and trade—or maybe the tools of the craft that has chosen me.

I go from town to town searching for people to hear words. Each evening they come—kindly, expectant, appreciative groups—to listen to this merchandiser of words. There is one problem that often occurs. It is that the crowds are too small. Now I don't mean that I have to have big audiences. I'm willing to run my words through their paces practically anywhere. That's not it. It is just that bigger audiences are safer. In a small group, you see, there is time to learn about the hurts and hopes that go along with the names. And in small groups I become more and more aware of how deep the need is for my words to be true.

I cannot just express my opinions or share a collection of

jokes and stories. So I find myself carefully going over my words in my room before I speak in the hope they will deserve being heard. Sometimes my words have needed to carry comfort and assurance and guidance to an eight-year-old boy whose mother just up and left the weekend before with another man. Sometimes they need to be said to a dedicated young lady who desperately wants to serve people but who is out of work. Once they were to a young professional whose wife died of cancer a few days before he was licensed to practice. There are times when I do not seem to have as many words at my command as I would like to have.

I am a writer of words, too—an author of published works, if you please. Being a lover of books, I was overjoyed one afternoon to see in the block next to where I was staying a three-story building that was labeled, THE BOOK EXCHANGE—THE SOUTH'S GREATEST BOOKSTORE. As soon as I could, I made my way into its shelf-lined innards. I don't believe I have ever seen as many books for sale in one place in my life. I was almost mesmerized—there were so many! There were new ones, old ones, used ones, discontinued ones, culls, cutouts, and seconds on what must have been every conceivable subject from every conceivable viewpoint.

"So you want to be a writer," I mumbled to myself. And just where in this vast graveyard of author's aspirations would you like for the remaindered editions of your works to be placed? On the second floor in the section marked Divinity Students? Or maybe down below in one of the many rooms through which the general reader can browse for bargains? Or to save the embarrassment of seeing the $7.95 crossed out on the dust jackets of your learned tomes and 75¢ penciled in, would you prefer to continue to buy them all yourself and keep force-feeding them to your garage until somehow it finally regurgitates them all?

A dealer in words? Why not automobiles, or lamps, or trees, or bedsheets, or anything but words? But my heart is hooked on words.

To help you believe that God has something to say to you I have to tell you that he has spoken to me. Always I have to talk about him from within the context of my life, for it has been in the daily round of my world that I have become increasingly aware of the speaking voice of God. The things I am saying about him, though, are universal. They express what he can mean to anyone. They are as true for every man as they are for me. They are sounding forth in your life as surely as they are in mine. Whoever you are and whatever your circumstances, he is the God who calls you. I believe these things about him, not because of who I am or what I have or of the places I have visited, but because of who he is and what he wants to be to everyone.

That's why I say to you as forcefully as I know how, "God has something to say to you!" I believe it for you because it has come to be true for me. Because I believe it, and since you have read this far, I am going to try seven other words on you.

You Can Hear Him If You Listen.

I am thinking just now of a hesitant comment made to me a few months ago. I know that it's not quite "cricket" to respond in a book to thoughts shared in an intense, private conversation. But maybe if the friend remains anonymous (and maybe if it is apparent that his question really belongs to all of us), I will be forgiven. I am just committing to paper the things I have been thinking and the things I wish I had thought to say at the time.

We were at a retreat surrounded by songs, scripture study, affirmation, and prayer—things that were laden with meaning for many of us there. But my friend was not feeling very religious and none of the things that were moving and touching the rest of us were making him feel anything at all. He confided that this frightened him.

I hastened to say that straw and altars and retreats and campmeeting singing had been a part of some of our lives for a long, long time. Meanings had accumulated around them for us until they are almost sacraments to us. But I could remember kneeling in the straw at an altar just like the one at which we were bowed. I had been sixteen at the time and I had stood up and gone out into the darkness dry-eyed and somewhat bewildered. But the decision I had made changed my life from that night forward.

Then came his wistful words—words that carried with them the longing to be aware of the presence of Christ, to know him in some deep way. "I just wish I could play tennis with him some afternoon," said my friend.

It's an old, old idea to think that it would be a lot easier to believe in God if you could see him. How do you explain that a God you cannot see is more real than one of whom you can take a picture? And how do you tell someone about a voice that cannot be audibly heard, yet conveys more truth and meaning than all the sounds crashing in on us all the time? How does one explain the simple but astonishing claim, "I know whom I have believed and am persuaded that he is able to keep that which I have committed unto him until that day"? How does one go about proving the reality of the kingdom?

Maybe it would help to begin with our definition of what *real* is. Real has come to mean something we can see, or touch, drive, eat, listen to, or wear. So we think that tennis is real. There is a racquet we can hold, a ball we can hit (or miss), sounds we can hear, lines we can contest, courts we can mark off and run, stumble and fall on, and rules we can print and read and jump up and down and scream over. (You have correctly observed that I have been watching John McEnroe.) Tennis matches can be watched and played and won and lost. So it must be a real game. But we have to be careful about our standards for real.

Norman Cousins, from his experiences at UCLA Medical School, describes the way we think about "real" and "unreal." He notes: "The words 'hard' and 'soft' are generally used by medical students to describe the contrasting nature of courses. Courses like biochemistry, physics, pharmacology, anatomy, and pathology are anointed with the benediction of 'hard,' whereas subjects like medical ethics, philosophy, history, and patient-physician relationships tend to labor under the far less auspicious label 'soft' . . . (but) a decade or two after graduation there tends to be an inversion. That which was supposed to be hard turns out to be soft, and vice versa. The knowledge base of medicine is constantly changing . . . . But the soft subjects—especially those that have to do with intangibles—turn out in the end to be of enduring value."[2]

It is an interesting statement, especially in the light of our views about what is real, that it is the intangibles which have enduring value. It reminds me of the title of a chapter in one of

Leo Buscaglia's books. He readily admits the phrase came to him from *The Little Prince* by Saint Exupery. The phrase is, "What is essential is invisible to the eye."

These are hard thoughts for us to grasp. To believe that the *invisible intangibles* are the *enduring essentials* is not the way we ordinarily think about things. It is a dramatic reversal to try to comprehend that if we can wear it, drive it, dance to it, drink it, touch it, count it, draw interest on it, live in it, or have it appraised, it is not essential. It will not endure. To begin to recognize that this so-called "soft" world is indeed the deepest reality one must begin to remember that values, honesty, faith, love, trust, hope, dignity, purpose, character (none of which can ever be seen with our eyes or held in our hands) are the real realities of our lives. Their true realness may be seen in their power to mold us when they are embraced. And it may be seen just as surely from the emptiness that results when we disdain them.

In Willa Cather's novel, *Death Comes for the Archbishop*, the bishop's friend, Father Vallient, remarks, "Doctrine is well enough for the wise, Jean, but the miracle is something we can hold in our hands and love." To which the Bishop replies, "The Miracles of the Church seem to me to rest not so much upon faces or voices or healing power coming suddenly near to us from afar off, but upon our perceptions being made finer, so that for a moment our eyes can see and our ears can hear what there is about us always."[3]

Maybe we need to know, too, that the reality of the kingdom is a discipline that can be learned. One must submit to its demands.

Tennis takes a racquet, a ball, shoes, a court, some skills, some energy, some aching muscles, some winning, some losing, and some recovery shots for match point after four hours in the afternoon sun. One doesn't get a racquet for his birthday and enter the U.S. Open. To get to know God also requires some time, some listening, some quiet, some discipline, some desire, however faltering our ways of hearing may seem to be at first.

The longing in our hearts is already the faint perception of the voice of God calling us. We could begin to acknowledge him even if it were only to ask him for some little thing that only he could give—some direction, some sense of purpose or inner help by which only we would know something had been accomplished. Maybe a simple "answer-me-if-you-are-there" kind of prayer is what we need to pray.

So I guess I really want to answer the longing, haunting questions of my friend. Is there anybody on the other side of the net? Will the ball come bouncing back to me if I smash it across the net? If I throw prayers into the sky will words come raining down around me? With all my heart, I want to tell him it is his serve. Go ahead and hit the ball. The silence will speak to you. The unseen will appear. The untouchable will grip you. The hidden will become visible. The unreachable can be reached. God has something to say to you and you can hear him if you listen.

He calls us—ceaselessly and persistently—in the conversations of others, through his Word, in the midst of trials and sicknesses, through books, and in myriads of other ways. God speaks to us.

In the introductory sentence of the Sermon on the Mount there is a most wonderful truth hidden in some very simple words, ". . . he opened his mouth, and taught them . . ." (Matthew 5:2 KJV). What a marvelous revelation. He talks to us. He will teach us. He is not a mute God. He is not a God whose ways are to remain unfathomable to us. We are not to spend our days forever wondering what he is thinking about and what it is he would like for us to do. He is a God who talks to us.

His words may be misinterpreted, and they often have been. They may be misunderstood, and many times they are. They may be misapplied, and it is almost certain they will be. They may be ignored, and they are. But still he talks to us.

It is precisely this inability of words to carry the same idea to everyone all the time that brings the deep meaning to this introductory line to his sermon on the mountain. For God to frame his will and intentions with the frailty of words should give us pause. Words can be misinterpreted and, worse yet, ignored; words can be redirected and changed by inflections and emphasis every time they are quoted. Bolts of lightning, maybe. Crashes of thunder, yes. Better still the winds of a tornado to get our attention. But words, just words, hardly seem enough.

Still God talks to us. It is a wonder that he would have something to say to us and a deeper wonder still that he would want to talk to us. And that from deep within him would come all the messages he has been wanting to tell us.

Robert Frost once told how poems came to him. He never succeeded in "larruping a poem like one might a horse to make it go." He said poems had come to him in their own ways: "A poem begins with a lump in the throat; a home-sickness or a love-sickness. It is a reaching out toward expression; an effort to find fulfillment. A complete poem is where an emotion has found its thought and the thought has found the words."[4] And sometimes poems take years to find the words.

It was more than just a young preacher teaching on a mountain that afternoon long ago. The deep longings of God, bottled up for so long, were now bursting forth from his heart.

"God has something to say to you!"

2

You Are the Framework of His Words

". . . think of what you were when you were called."

1 Corinthians 1:26

We are not numbers to Him; we are persons intimately known. We are His, in the only way we can be His, namely by His knowledge of ourselves that differentiates us from all the others. He will be our guide in this the determinative quest for our real self. He comes to us, each one, saying, "Follow Me, and you will find your real self."

Albert Edward Day[1]

2
You Are the Framework
of His Words

When Mom and Dad brought me home for the first time from
the old Saint Thomas Hospital, it was to a modest house out in
east Nashville across the street from the old Trevecca College
Campus. While I did not realize it at the time, the college had
already begun an influence on me which I guess is to be lifelong.

Mother had left her home as a young girl to go down to
Donalsonville, Georgia, to a small holiness school. But almost as
she was arriving, the school entered the final throes of going
under. My paternal grandfather, John T. Benson, Sr., visited the
campus and invited all the students to come to Nashville. He
extended the warmth and hospitality of Trevecca College to
them all. He offered my mother student employment in the
cafeteria to help her pay her way.

Neither of them realized at the time that the hospitality would
also come to include his youngest son, John, first as sweetheart
and later as husband, a home for the first year of their married
life in the Benson household up on Gallatin Pike, and then the
house at 945 McClurkan Avenue.

The small, white frame house to which I was taken to live

25

was one of many built in Old Hickory during the First World War to house the flood of laborers who came to work in the Dupont Powder Plant. Grandfather Benson bought the house and had it moved a dozen or so miles to the lot across from the old administration building at the eastern edge of the campus.

My earliest recollections come back to me from the first six years of my life spent there. My memories are, like yours, an odd assortment of sights, sounds, mishaps, people and incidents.

I remember taking naps in the back bedroom with the old Emerson electric fan slowly oscillating back and forth between my bed and my sister Laura's. Later on, in our new home out on Brush Hill (when my brother John and I would lie awake on hot summer nights waiting for the fan to come back from the other side), I decided the height of opulence and prosperity would be to have a fan that did not have to swing back and forth. A fan whose sole purpose was to remain steadfastly directed toward you and you alone.

I remember lots of the neighbors because the people from the church began to move into the neighborhood around the college. Many of their children and their children's children—and their children as well—are still a part of my life. The Gunns, the Sloneckers, the Moores, the Matthews and many more. I remember one lady, Mrs. Opie, especially because she would give Laura and me brown sugar to eat when we slipped across the alley to visit her. Even these many years later, I still think being offered a bowl of brown sugar is a most civil custom.

My brother John is almost three years older than I and Mom recalls that he was looking forward to having a little brother to play with. But when she brought me home, he suddenly realized that all I was big enough to do was eat and sleep and cry. The girl next door had a cousin who could play out in the yard so John wanted them to exchange me for a cousin.

John ran around with such worldly characters as Gilbert Roberts and Brooks Duncan. One afternoon John and Brooks ran away from home and were finally found over on Straightway Avenue nearly to Eastland School. The sounds emerging from the garage that evening, where he and Dad had gone to discuss the matter of crossing Gallatin Pike and the streetcar tracks, served to introduce me at a very young age to the causes of right and obedience.

It was those two scamps, John and Brooks, who steered me into about the only fight I ever remember winning. I can't recall my opponent or the circumstances but I can still show you the exact spot at the corner of Strouse and Trevecca Avenue where I bloodied his nose with a blow that stopped the bout. It was such a mighty lick that it would not surprise me at all to find the stains of blood still there on the pavement.

It was somewhere along there that I put the first blemish on my own body also. (Unfortunately, it was not going to be the last.) I was perched on the kitchen stool, which was always called the high stool at our house, eating chocolate ice cream. I must have been eating it too fast. It has never been hard for me to eat ice cream too fast. And I fainted and fell on the enamel-topped table and split my chin open. Mom ran up the street and got Myrt Slonecker and they took me up to Bunches Clinic in Myrt's car to have me sewn up. It was a sobering experience to first realize that your very own skin will tear open and that you can leak out of yourself unless you are sewn back together again. The only thing worse has been going along as a father when one of your children makes the same woeful discovery. I have sat in on the repair of enough cuts and tears and fishhook removals to be sure that this is true.

I made several early decisions about what I wanted to be when I grew up. Each one was shaped by the people who were part of neighborhood life in the early thirties. For awhile I wanted to be a vegetable man like the one who drove his pa-tient, drowsy horse pulling the heavily laden wagon down the street in front of our house. And then it was to be an iceman—like the man who looked at the card in our window and then according to the number at the top chipped off the size block we needed that day. While he was carrying the ice to the house he would let the kids climb up and eat the slivers that had fallen on the cool, moist wood of the truck bed.

As a husband I hate to admit this, but for a time I even thought of being a trash man. But a few trips to town on the street car turned my intentions from waste disposal and to the more official-looking job of motorman. Then all of that changed the day I was playing in the front yard and heard the siren of the firetruck coming out the Pike and watched it turn onto McClurkan and roar by our house. It was only a vacant lot on fire but I knew then that I was cut out for a life of excitement. I wasn't sure whether I wanted to drive the firetruck or hang on the back—but that was a choice I could make later. Even to this day, when a firetruck goes flying past me I wonder if I missed my calling. At least if it is a red one. I never have been sure about the chartreuse ones (or anything else that color for that matter). Even now it seems that there were a lot more interesting occupations back then.

It is interesting the things that one remembers, the things that are suddenly recalled from long, long ago. I can still hear the soft purring of that fan while we took our nap. I can still see the firetruck turning into McClurkan as if it were this morning. I'm sure the experiences that have stayed with me are not the same as those my parents recall about those days, or the recollections of John or Laura.

Of course, there are some events that are sort of common property because they are part of the family legends and lore. Like the time Dad hit his toe when he was crushing ice to make homemade ice cream. It may not have happened exactly as I remember, but I can still see him holding his injured foot as high as he could. He was hopping around the house on his other foot so fast that no one could catch him to see how badly he was injured.

We Are Distinct and Different

A person's montage of memories and impressions are peculiarly and particularly his own. The things which I recall from the "olden days," as my children irreverently call them now, are gathered up in a shape and form that is mine alone. They are part of what makes me *me*. My collection of memories, actions, reactions, prejudices, hangups, accomplishments, defeats, gifts and weaknesses is not quite like anyone else's anywhere.

Of course I am not alone in this. You, too, have your collection of memories and impressions and feelings from the past. Rilke, the German poet, in advising a younger friend, told him to write out of the experiences that were his own. He reminded him of the rich sources hidden within. "If your daily life seems poor, do not blame it; blame yourself. Tell yourself that you are not poet enough to call forth its riches; for to the Creator there is no poverty and no poor indifferent place. And even if you were in some prison the walls of which let none of the sounds of the world come to your senses—would you not then still have your childhood, that precious kingly possession, that treasure house of memories?"[2]

His Words Are Personal

Each of our treasure houses is different. They give each one of us an inner silhouette and contour that is varied and separate. It is this very diversity which gives me occasion to think of the wonder of God's calling to us, and of the marvel of his grace as it comes to us. Since we are each so obviously different and distinct, it becomes apparent that his call must be intensely personal. It sounds out to us in a melody that only we can perfectly hear. For it plays out of our own personalities, our own backgrounds, our own hopes and dreams, our own gifts. It is uniquely ours.

Elizabeth-Paul Labat, a Benedictine nun who lived and died in France, wrote a lovely book about the presence of God. Writing about his coming to us through his grace she tells us, "It is a reality that is invisible in itself, like the God from whom it comes. It is also so modest and adaptable that it never goes beyond the limits of the nature that it perfects. It is finally so powerful and effective that it allows us to perform actions that are both human and divine and transfigures us to such a degree that we become gods by participation, sons of God in the one Son and the fullness of the spirit."[3]

No wonder that when we speak and sing of the calling grace of God we use the word "amazing." Coming to us in such a myriad of shapes and forms, it reaches into the corners and crannies that have been hollowed out by time and experience in our one-of-a-kind hearts.

I think there are two ways one can find the real significance of this calling voice of God. First, a person can take the advice of us oldtimers and "just let go and let God." That's the way we did it and that's the reason we think it is the way you should do it also. Just believe what we are telling you about him and jump in. And we promise you that if you do he will catch you. If you will trust his promises, you will find that they are all true, that he indeed is who he says he is and that he can do what he says he can do. And when you find him, you will have also found yourself. For you are a part of his reality.

But that's not always so easy, is it? Reason argues against trusting yourself to a God you cannot see, leaping by faith over a chasm when the other side seems so far away. I would suggest that there is another way to come to God—by coming to your own true self. Discover the essential movement of your life. It will be as Saint John Chrysostom said, "Find the door of your heart and you will find the door of the kingdom of heaven."

Evelyn Underhill, the famous English mystical writer of the early twentieth century believed that "we spend most of our lives conjugating three verbs: to Want, to Have, and to Do." She may have been right, because it seems we do spend much of our lives in a state of constant unrest governed by craving, grasping, and frenzied activity. She also notes that ". . . none of these verbs have any ultimate significance, except so far as they are transcended by and included in, the fundamental verb, to Be: and that Being, not wanting, having, doing, is the essence of spiritual life."[4]

It is when one comes to know who he truly is to be that the "to wants," and the "to haves," and the "to dos" begin to take their proper place. And the answer to who we are and what we are to be is found in God's calling voice to us.

It will no doubt take some real effort on our part to begin to discover who it is that we really are. We are all so conditioned by the world in which we live that we can go a lifetime and never get within a stone's throw of our own true selves. Though it will be difficult, it is necessary to try to clear away much of the debris society places about us. Things like status, opinions of others, conformity and peer pressures which can keep us from examining the real touchstones of life will have to be forgotten for a moment. We will have to sense our hopes and our feelings about people, purposes, occupations. We will have to ask ourselves some pointed, revealing questions. Questions like these: "Do I like what I am doing enough to spend a lifetime doing it? Is this the opportunity to be involved with others and with life in a way that I feel good about? What would I really like to be doing? What do I really want in life? What do I see myself as in my dreams? Who do I most deeply sense that I am?"

It will take some time for us to come to ourselves. But when we do, when the deep, real part of us has spoken, we will have come to God. Because this best part of us—our finest aspirations, our highest hopes and dreams, our noblest intentions and purest desires—these are the image of God within us. They are his calling to us from deep within the springs of our own beings.

Hearing This Personal Call

I am not sure exactly what all I think we mean when we say that we are all made in the image of God. But part of it, I am coming to believe, is that the calling voice of God is sounding out in the caves and caverns deep beneath the soil of our souls. And that it is by obeying this call that we learn who we truly are and what we can become.

So if I do not seem to hear him speak from the outside and if there does not seem to be any message from the sky, then I must listen to the voice that is within me. For that voice, too, is the purposeful, calling voice of God to us.

Paul tells us to ". . . think of what we were when we were called." Part of what he is suggesting is that this is one of the best ways of bringing into focus the sometimes seemingly faint outlines of his calling to us. We can begin by bringing our own hearts and lives under careful remembrance and scrutiny. To think of what we were will very likely make us aware that we are the very framework of his calling to us. It is to begin to believe for ourselves the words of Isaiah:

> God called me before I was born,
> from my mother's womb he pronounced my name.
> Isaiah 49:1

Not many of us have enough confidence in ourselves to listen to the whispering voice that comes from within. We do not even hear it. But it does not matter because we wouldn't trust it. We cannot believe that this inner voice is capable of leading us due

north. We seek advice and counsel from friends and profession-
als—and disc jockeys and Dear Abbys. We put out a fleece. We
flip coins. We take aptitude tests. We do everything but believe
that we could possibly have the answers deep within.

The message of Paul in this place is that the calling indeed
comes in the lives of the unlikely and the "foolish." You think
you are unlikely; well you're not. You have difficulty believing
that God could do great things in you; well, he wouldn't.

Early last spring, I was reminded again that this is true. I was
planting my garden. It was late on a Thursday evening and I
was leaving the next morning for ten days of travel and speaking so I was hurrying to finish before the darkness came. I had
run out of sticks to mark the rows, and was about to go to the
kindling box in the garage and get some more so the beds
would be neatly marked and labeled. Then I suddenly wondered why I needed the labels anyway. By the time I would get
back, the plants would be up and I could see where they were
growing. From experience, I knew that the rabbits knew which
kind of vegetables they liked. And I sure knew that I knew peas
from spinach. And the seeds sure knew what they were. Who
needed labels? So I just covered the seeds with the cool, moist
earth and gently patted the beds down and said, "Go ahead and
sprout. You know what you are. I'll see you in a few days when
I get back." And they did, and I did.

Now if God can take a tiny seed and in the process of giving
it his life endow it with a knowledge of what it is supposed to
be; if he can give it the purpose and strength and fruitfulness to
not only accomplish it all, but to perpetuate itself as well; and if
he can give it an inner calendar to tell it when all of this is
supposed to be done—why should it be so hard for us to believe he has done the same within our hearts? Since he has done
this for tomatoes and thistles and beans and dandelions, it
should not stretch our credibility so much to believe that his
image in us, the image inherent in the life he gives to each of us,
is calling us to be. And when we truly become we will be very
near to him.

The trick is to hear the voice, to believe it, and to trust it. In
her book, *Teaching a Stone to Talk*, Annie Dillard, brilliant con-
temporary writer, tells of going to Hollins Pond late in the afternoon. Hollins Pond is about twenty minutes from her house and

it "covers two acres of bottomland near Tinker creek with six inches of water and six thousand lily pads." She goes there, as indeed she goes many places in the world, to ". . . remember how to live," because she would like to "live as she should." And she reminds us, in her own poignant way, that the "thing is to stalk your calling in a certain skilled and supple way, to locate the most tender and live spot and plug into that pulse." Further, she writes, "I think it would be well, and proper, and obedient, and pure, to grasp your one necessity and not let it go . . . ."5

Maybe her two phrases, "stalk your calling" and "grasp your one necessity" give us some idea of the shape of the quest that must be undertaken if we are to hear the voice within. Words like stalk and grasp and necessity tell us that this is a task which will make demands on us. Demands for diligence, for stillness, for singlemindedness. But words like that also tell us it is a quest that will amply reward us upon completion—that it is a quest worthy of being our highest goal.

We usually define sin as a refusal to do something that we know God commands or wills us to do or else as a determination to do something which we know he forbids. Tom Merton, the late writer-monk, had a different view. He wrote, "Sin is the refusal of spiritual life, the rejection of the inner order and peace that come from our union with the divine will." In reality, Merton concluded, sin is "more radically a refusal to be what we are, a rejection of our mysterious, contingent, spiritual reality hidden in the very mystery of God. Sin is our refusal to be what we were created to be—sons of God, images of God."6

It has been my intention as a parent to believe in and respect the specialness of the calling of God in the hearts and lives of my children. I think I can accurately be described as a "nondirective" parent. I'm not sure that this is always necessarily the best—and I'm not sure altogether how I came to be this way. Part of the reason is my natural readiness to avoid confrontation if I can. Part of the reason is that I want to believe everything will work out for everybody.

Then, I think, too, that I got caught in the way the generations swing back and forth in their manner of parenting. I remember one day when my dad and I were walking along on Church Street in front of Harvey's Department Store. I noticed a plaque in the sidewalk which noted the paving had been done in 1927, and I asked Dad if he had walked over this same spot with his father in days gone by. He said he didn't think so. Because he had been the last child in a large family, he had always felt his dad was tired of children by the time he came along. So he didn't remember their walking many places together. Thinking that his father had not been as prominent in his life as he would have liked for him to have been, my dad decided early on that he would get involved in the lives of his children.

For instance, he was an expert at knowing things like where you were supposed to go to college. I didn't have to spend a lot of time deliberating where to pursue my education after high school. Quite simply, I went to the place where he was sending the tuition money. I graduated from high school one night at 8:00 and caught the 10:30 bus. The next morning I was 220 miles away in freshman Greek class at Asbury College. As I said, my dad got involved in the lives and decisions of his children.

Maybe this accounts in some measure for my hanging back and encouraging my five to make up their own minds. One of them will come to me and say, "What should I do about this?" And I will try to look as wise as I can. I will pause significantly, as fathers will do, indicating that I am deep in thought about the matter. Then I make a studied and weighty pronouncement. Most of the time I profoundly answer, "I dunno."

I am not at all convinced that this is a superior way of parenting. Already some of my sons are old enough to look back and point to given moments in their lives when they needed more direction than their father was able or willing to provide. But I have earnestly believed, and tried to get my children to believe, that if they listened to the quiet voice within they would know the answer, because a part of his image within them is his calling voice.

There have been some times when the temptation as a father has been to assume that it would be best to just go ahead and tell my children what they should do. Still, there was something that kept me from doing this. Maybe it was because I always somehow knew that I could not necessarily know what was right for a given child.

All of your children live in the same house and they ride in the same car and eat the same cereal for breakfast. They sometimes even wear the same hand-me-down tennis shoes. Your children have the same last name and the same parents. But your children are not the same. Not at all. Each one is unique. There are no "boiler plate" clauses that fit all children. They are like snowflakes with their own patterns and their own shapes and their own sizes. They have their own places to land. So their calling must come at precisely the right time and in the right way. They alone can hear the call of the One who can tell them what to be. And I cannot make them be tomatoes when they were destined to be radishes. Or scholars if they were meant to be farmers. Or accountants if what they really want to be poets.

Kahlil Gibran expresses my truest feelings about all this when he writes:

> Your children are not your children.
> They are the sons and daughters of Life's longing for itself.
> They come through you but not from you,
> And though they are with you yet they belong not to you.
>
> You may give them your love but not your thoughts,
> For they have their own thoughts.
> You may house their bodies but not their souls,
> For their souls dwell in the house of tomorrow, which you
>   cannot visit, not even in your dreams.
> You may strive to be like them, but seek not to make them like
>   you.
> For life goes not backward nor tarries with yesterday.
> You are the bows from which your children as living arrows are
>   sent forth.[7]

As a parent, I have decided that I can't do or decide or discern everything. But I can live like one who has heard the voice that called him. And I can love. And I can pray. And I can hope. And I can occasionally give advice. I can tell my children that there is a voice which will speak to them. I can even drop hints. I can remind them (and have) that they could hear the inner voice better if they turned the stereo down, or better still, off altogether. I can say that the most important thing in life is to hear and obey the voice. And I can say that the gravest danger in all of life is to fail to hear and heed the voice. But I cannot tell them what it will say to them. For the call that is within them is just to them.

M. Basil Pennington, a Trappist monk from Spencer, Massachusetts, tells a good story about a Syrian rabbi whose name was Zuscha. On his deathbed someone asked him what he thought the kingdom of God was going to be like. The old rabbi thought for quite a while and then he gave his answer. "I really don't know. But one thing I do know; When I get there, I am not going to be asked, 'Why weren't you Moses?' or 'Why weren't you David?' I am going to be asked, 'Why weren't you Zuscha?' "[8]

He is right. The calling of God is personal. It comes from within you and it is to you. And it is calling for you to be you.

3

A Way to Live on Purpose

"And those he predestined, he also called . . ."

ROMANS 8:30

(The attempt to follow Christ) ". . . does not consist in engaging in propaganda, not even in stirring people up, but in being a living mystery. It means to live in such a way that one's own life would not make sense if God did not exist."

CARDINAL SUHARD[1]

3

A Way to Live on Purpose

Several months ago, I moved my office across Nashville from Madison to Brentwood. It shortened a journey of some forty miles round trip to one of just over three. Since that move I have made one more which established my office upstairs in the back of our home. And that made the three-mile trip a stroll down the hall.

Leaving Madison was kind of a final break with the side of town in which I had lived most of my life until this present house. When I was growing up in east Nashville, Madison was just a wide place in the road with a few stores and a theater that showed westerns on Saturday afternoons. However, the five- or six-mile journey out there held all kinds of adventure, especially if you were riding on your bicycle. Maybe it was partly because I wasn't really supposed to ride my bike on Gallatin Pike anyway.

From our house you followed Brush Hill as it ran along the Cumberland River bluff and then turned down Log Cabin Road until you came to Haysboro and then the "pike" as everyone in our neighborhood called it. You turned north there and soon were riding between two cemeteries. Springhill is on the east side of the pike and my paternal grandparents are buried there. My dad told me that his mother picked out the lot about a block inside the new gate and had the big, simple tombstone marked Benson erected over my grandfather's grave. Dad said that someone in the family told her that it seemed noisy there so close to the main road, but my grandmother remarked that she couldn't hear out of one ear anyway and it would be all right for her when her time came. I was so young when I was riding through the cemetery with my friends on our bicycles that it never dawned on me my time was going to come sometime too. On the other side of the road is the National Cemetery and there aren't any of us Bensons buried over there since we never have produced many fighters. Both cemeteries had shady, winding roads that beckoned to be ridden on and explored before going on over the hill and into Madison. The graveyard for the soldiers had a thick, high wall around it and it was a test of courage to ride on it. It was not for the faint-hearted, but I think I have ridden on it (and off of it too).

So it was with some sadness that I drove the rental truck filled with my books, shelves, antique tables, pictures and John F. Lawhon couch and chair away from the Madison Building. But I was looking forward to getting all my stuff set up in my new office or "office suite" as the landlord had called it when I had inquired about renting it. I have always loved an office. In our first pastorate after seminary I could hardly wait to get my office fixed up. However, since the new congregation in Modesto, California, did not have its own building we had to rent a place to worship. Initially we met in the front of a former feedstore and later on in a community clubhouse. Since neither had office space for a young parson I divided our part of the garage with refrigerator crates to have a place to get up and go to in the mornings. The garage for the duplex had already been divided once and a rising young foot doctor made plaster moulds of his patient's feet in the other side of it.

It was hot and dusty in the summer and cold and clammy in the winter, but I steadfastly maintained office hours (although it never seemed quite fitting that a fiery prophet should be preparing his messages in a Kelvinator crate).

So in Brentwood I fell joyfully to the task of unpacking my books and arranging and rearranging the furniture as Patrick (my youngest son) and Patrick (one of his biggest friends) hauled it all up the hall and into my new quarters. I am one of those people who actually likes to shift furniture around. I came by this quite honestly because my mother was and is a confirmed furniture mover. She belongs to the school that holds that furniture was made to be moved, and further, that there is no way of knowing how the piano will look over by the other wall until you move it over there and see. Fortunately, my wife Peggy is a rearranger also. And at times when it seems as if our lives are sinking slowly away into the doldrums we will often begin our escape by moving the living room furniture around.

When the furniture was all in and the books were back on the shelves it was time to hang my pictures and stuff on the walls. This is a project in itself because over the years I have accumulated an amazing array of things to hang around me. It is almost as if when we did not know quite what to do with something we just had it framed and put it on the wall somewhere. There are pictures, macrames, paintings, plaques, certificates, diplomas, logos, poems, mottos, awards, cartoons and a brass plate proclaiming "Confessions Held 5:00 to 7:00 Daily." And now all of these items were clamoring to be displayed in a manner befitting their importance.

The pictures are the easiest to hang because for the most part they aren't of me except in a group or on a team. They are of family and friends at various stages and ages. Then I always hesitate a little with the diplomas and the degrees. They seem a trifle ostentatious, to say the least. Usually, though, my need to appear important overcomes my need to be humble and I mix them in as unobtrusively as I can here and there. As E. B. White has correctly observed, the plaques and trophies give you the most trouble. In my more reflective moments I am aware that it is probably a little much for some group or organization to have publicly proclaimed, much less to have engraved in bronze, that I was or am or will be "an outstanding Christian leader"—or some other phrase equally heartwarming to me. But they do have a nice ring to them. Since they are impressive metal plaques mounted on rich mahogany-finished bases, it seems a shame to throw them away. And anyway, somebody else said all those things. I just am not sure I ought to keep on posting them since I am so thoroughly familiar with the facts.

When I get all my stuff up, I am home. For they are all mine—collected, framed, bought, received—and they are the things that make a place mine whether it is a refrigerator crate or an "office suite." They are a sort of a running account of the places I have been, the things I have done, the people I have loved, and gifts from people who have said they loved me.

Searching for a Plot

Somehow all of this, my office and the things occupying its walls, not to mention my heart and all that its surfaces are covered with, came to mind recently as I was reading Evelyn Underhill's *Abba*, her lovely little book on the Lord's Prayer. She was commenting on the four word phrase, "Hallowed be thy name" and she wrote ". . . this petition can cover, criticize, and re-interpret the whole of our personal life; cleansing it from egotism . . . and reminding us that our life and work are without significance, except insofar as they glorify God to whom nothing is adequate but everything is dear."[2] And I was reminded that there is an all-pervading purpose around which we may cluster all that we do and say and try to accomplish. I cannot think of anything more frightening about life than to have lived it without any real reason. Certainly I am not alone in wondering about how to find true meaning.

I was reading about Renata Adler the other day and how she wrote her first novel, *Speedboat*. Ms. Adler is a reviewer having written columns for *The New York Times* and *The New Yorker*. She also had published books before the novel, but they were collections of her previous essays and reviews. At first she thought her new book would be a collection of short stories rather than a novel. Then she decided perhaps there was a novel in there somewhere. So she continued to work "waiting for a plot to emerge."

In a more philosophical tone she added, "I used to think that at some point you'd see your life as a long narrative swing, that at some point you could see the shape of things and all the different strands would come together. Now, I don't. You can find a plot to a week or a couple of days, but not much more, not to a lifetime."[3]

It did not seem altogether proper to me that she felt a responsibility to provide her characters with a plot by which to live when she did not sense one present in her own life. It seems to me that it *is* possible to find the central thread around which each of our lives is woven. In fact, I believe the longer I live the more it seems that all the stepping stones are indeed heading in one direction. Even places that at one time looked like detours at best, or dead-end roads at their worst, appear now to have moved me along to where I am.

However, I do think Renata Adler is accurate in describing the way many of us spend much of our time when she observes that we spend our days "waiting for the plot to emerge." For lurking beneath everyone's days and hours there are, and always have been, the questions of the meaning of things. It was Saint Augustine who wrote:

> The very order
> disposition, beauty, change
> and the motion of the world and
> of all visible things,
> silently proclaim
> that it could only have been
> made by God
> the ineffably and invisibly Great
> and the ineffably and invisibly
> Beautiful.

His words are quite a contrast to those of Irwin Shaw who entitled a book, *God Was Here, But He Left Early*. Or to those of Clarence Day, who wrote about his father, "Father expected a good deal of God. He didn't actually accuse God of inefficiency, but when he prayed his tone was loud and angry, like that of a dissatisfied guest in a carelessly managed hotel."[4] Different answers, but the questions are always alive and always the same.

When one begins to think about the purposes of God and his working in the events in the lives of men and women, probably no verse of scripture comes more quickly to mind than the gracious words of Romans 8:28, "And we know that in all things God works for the good of those who love him, who have been called according to his purpose." These words are imbedded in my memory from long ago.

My dad sponsored a campmeeting for several years at a place called Ruskin Cave down in west Tennessee. One of the great oldtime preachers whom he invited back year after year was Raymond Browning. Brother Browning was a powerful preacher who stirred a certain amount of fear in the heart of a teenager. He was also such a marvelous storyteller that you did not want to miss the morning services in which he spoke. Two of his sermons became favorites over the years and he was asked to deliver them again and again. One of them was from Exodus 4:2 when God asked Moses, "What is that in thine hand?" And the other was from Romans 8:28. Brother Browning was a big, distinguished man whose head was covered with snowy white hair. When he preached from the Exodus verse, we were not quite sure whether he looked more like Moses or more like God. But we knew it was one of the two (if not both). And when he spoke from Romans 8:28 we could just feel the majesty and power radiate from the promise that God was working out everything for our good. Brother Browning had gone to school under old Sawney Webb down at Bell Buckle, Tennessee, and he was a great scholar and a fluent, flawless speaker. It is to his credit that these words of Romans 8:28 have a beauty and meaning almost like poetry to all of us who heard him those lovely summer mornings.

So it is natural for me to turn to this verse in Romans when I think of the calling of God to us all. To tell you the truth, I wanted to use nearly all of the rest of the chapter. I thought of the deep meaning of such phrases as "If God be for us, who can be against us?" and "Who shall separate us from the love of Christ?" and "No, in all these things we are more than conquerors through him who loved us" and then conclude with Paul's ringing climax that "nothing will be able to separate us from the love of God that is in Christ Jesus our Lord."

Unfortunately for us Wesleyan-type theologians, stuck right in the middle of all these verses that give us so much hope and comfort there is this twenty-ninth verse. It is not one to which we often turn for preaching material. It is studded with words that we are not accustomed to using—words like "foreknew" and "predestine." We hardly ever preach on the foreknowledge of God, and never, ever on predestination.

I had been introduced to both of these words in college and

seminary. In both places, we young theologs had engaged in endless and learned debates about the foreknowledge of God. If God knows something is going to happen in a certain way, then it can't happen any other way; and if it can't happen any other way, then how can we be held responsible? And if we can't be held responsible for our choices, since we were predestined to make them anyway, then why should we worry about it?

Frankly, I don't think we ever arrived at an answer that fully reconciled these weighty matters with the other equally weighty ones of free will and personal responsibility. To be even franker, I don't recall our professors giving us a definitive answer either.

I will have to admit that I approached these two verses still looking for an Arminian angle. And I must also admit that the angle was harder to find than it is in other verses we often quote (where Paul wrote about the freedom of the human will and about our responsibility and need for repentance and faith and love). And these must not be forgotten.

But in these particular verses, Paul is describing the majestic movement of God in which the successive stages of his purposes are carried out. Paul does not even mention the activity of the believer. Here, he is thinking about the actions of God. And since ultimately all of our hope and our thanksgiving rests here anyway, Paul calls us to consider the mysterious, loving, eternal purpose of God.

He writes of the divine purpose which is being carried into effect. First, it begins in an act of divine intelligence which reaches back into eternity. God "foreknew" us, and even then he loved us and regarded us with his favor. It is further expressed as an act of divine will. For those he foreknew he "predestined" to be made into the image of his Son. And this deep purpose of God which began in eternity is brought into the reality of time by the divine call. "Those he predestined, he also called." Finally, there is the act of divine forgiveness by which we are justified. It is evident, to Paul at least, that the future glory of the believer is a present reality in the mind and purpose of God.

The gracious promise contained in Romans 8:28 has always been a source of comfort and aid, and it is still a favorite verse of Christians. But there are two conditions implicit in its words that give access to the blessings it promises. The first is the human response. It is a promise made to those who "love" God. The other condition has to do with the divine initiative. It is given to those who are "called according to his purpose." And it is for this reason we must turn to the twenty-ninth verse, for it is here that the "purpose" is stated for us. The purpose is contained in a process by which we are to become more and more like his Son. This is the watershed of every theology, for it is the eternal purpose of God—our conformity to his Son.

Popular evangelist, pastor, and writer Stuart Briscoe wrote in the volume on Romans of *The Communicator's Commentary* that Romans 8:28 is not ". . . to be seen as grounds for believing that 'everything will come out in the wash' because God has committed himself to sorting out the mess of our lives and relieving us of the consequences of our actions. It is eternal rather than temporal good which God has in mind. He works 'according to His purpose,' which is far grander than the alleviation of the unpleasantness of the present or a guarantee of plain sailing under cloudless skies in the foreseeable future. He is in the 'good' business of making redeemed sinners like their elder brother, the Lord Jesus, and even a cursory glance at the way the Father exposed the Son to the realities of life and death should be sufficient to remind us that we can expect the same kind of processes to work in our lives with the identical and ultimate result—conformity to Him."[5]

This is a deep, foundational truth. God's purposes are eternal rather than temporal. And if we ever expect to see the "plot emerge" it will have to be as we begin to acknowledge that God is the writer of the script. We have to understand that the point of the plot is that we be "conformed to the likeness of his Son." All he has done for us in the past, all he is doing now on our behalf, and all he has planned to do for us is in accordance with his purpose that we should be like his Son. Maybe we could begin to cooperate with the process better if we understood what it is that he wants to accomplish in us and through us.

Sticking to the Script

It is probably true that most of our perplexity does not come from the fact that the plot to our lives has not yet seemed to emerge. More likely, it springs from our notion that the script needs some revision. The other day I saw a book with a most intriguing title, *A Whack on the Side of the Head.* It contained a little article that pointed this out to me. It had to do with our natural desire to become scriptwriters and was entitled "Life is Lived All Backwards."

> I think that the life cycle is
> all backwards. You should die first,
> get it out of the way, then live
> twenty years in an old age home. You
> get kicked out when you're too
> young, you get a gold watch,
> you go to work. You work forty
> years until you're young enough to
> enjoy your retirement.
>
> You go to college. . . . until
> you're ready for high school. You
> go to grade school, you become a little
> kid, you play, you have no
> responsibilities, you become a
> little baby, you go back into
> the womb, you spend your last nine
> months floating, and you finish
> off as a gleam in somebody's
> eye.[6]

If the purpose for our lives is to be happier and happier and easier and easier then it is probably true that it is all "backwards." It certainly would fit into the great American dream better if life were lived in the other direction. But in the stately purposes of God we are led through life in a way that will finally bring us to our true destiny. That still doesn't seem to keep us from always wanting to tinker with the script.

I was watching religious television the other morning, although it doesn't always make me feel religious. But I was alone and away from home and I had the whole day to spend before speaking in the evening. And it certainly beat what was being shown on the nonreligious channels at the time.

I think the program was hosted by a couple from the West Coast. I had never seen them before and I did not know them, but in all fairness they probably still have never seen me and don't know who I am either. They were accepting calls from all over the country from viewers who were phoning in to ask the hosts to pray with them for specific answers to various needs and problems. The hosts would agree to "agree" with the caller and then take the petition to God.

One lady phoned in and was describing some very pressing matters in her life. After her needs were presented, the host indicated it was time to pray. Not being a regular viewer, I was not sure whether the next expression he used was a common one to him or not. But it seemed to be rather unfortunate to me. At least it was a phrase that I would not have thought of using in connection with praying. For after a few moments, one of the hosts said, "Well, let's go for it!"

In defense of the term I'm sure I am far too reticent to ask the Father for all I should be asking for or for all that he wants me to. Further, I am usually careful not to get myself into situations that will graphically and immediately demonstrate my prowess as a warrior in prayer. But still, "Let's go for it" seems more like something you would expect to hear on "Let's Make A Deal" when someone is choosing between the $5000 and the Cadillac. Anyway, they went for it.

I think one of the reasons why this example of prayer stuck in my mind was that I had recently heard a very profound and moving sermon on prayer by my friend, Paul Garlington. At one point, he was speaking about the matter of "agreeing" with one another about a particular promise, and then notifying the Father that for him to do any less than exactly what we asked would somehow leave him breaking his own word. I don't think this preacher was decrying our getting fellow believers to pray with us for an answer. I also don't think he was remotely suggesting God would break his promises to us. He was instead pointing out a deep way of approaching our heavenly Father in trust and obedience.

To illustrate what he meant, he asked the congregation if we remembered what it was that Jesus prayed when he stood before the five thousand hungry people with five loaves and two fish in his hands. In his own style, for Garlington is as dramatic as he is profound, he reminded us that Jesus did not wrinkle his brow and pray in a voice laden with earnestness and fervor, "Father, we need a miracle! And we are believing You for it just now." Instead Jesus had the people seat themselves on the hillside, and then he bowed his head and simply prayed, "Thank You."

Garlington went on to ask if we remembered the prayer of Jesus when he stood at the tomb of Lazarus. Again, to make the utter simplicity of the words of Jesus more powerful, he told us some of the things Jesus did not pray. He did not ask for a few true believers to join hands and "agree" with him that this was what they wanted the Father to do. Instead, Jesus, standing in front of the tomb from which the stone had just been rolled away and out of which the stench of death was streaming, looked up to his Father and said, "Thanks. I thank You that You hear me. And I thank You that You always hear me and even now I am only saying this so those who stand here with me will know You hear me."

Jesus did not seem to need anyone to agree with him in prayer. He and the Father already had an "agreement." The agreement was the Father's will, leaving Jesus remarkably free to lift his heart and voice in thanksgiving and praise: "Thanks, if You can make this food to go around. Thanks, if we all have to go home hungry. Thanks, if You raise Lazarus from the dead. Thanks, if we all leave this burial place with our hearts heavy with grief from the loss of our friend and brother. Thanks for Your will. Thanks for Your purpose. Thanks."

Jess Lair, the university professor who loves to use the word "ain't" in all his book titles, quotes a friend named Vince in one of his books. Vince's wisdom in *Ain't I a Wonder and Ain't You a Wonder Too!* is, "If I want to live the abundant life, I've got to stop fighting for complete control. If you want to live abundantly, you must surrender. There ain't no money nor job nor power that can help you get rid of grief. You've got to accept God or be God." And Jess remarked, "That is the simplest I've ever heard the matter put. You've got to accept some higher power, some power outside yourself or you've got to be it. When you try being God, you're all the power there is."[7]

That's the great difficulty in trying to be our own god. Even when we think we know what should be done (and most of the time we don't) we are powerless to bring it about. We do not have the power to change many things, people or circumstances. Most of the time, we can't even change ourselves. As

Jess said, "I'm powerless in the important things of my life. I can change a tire but I can't change my personality."[8]

And so we need a God who can. But what is so hard to acknowledge is that in all likelihood, the God who has the power to do what needs to be done also knows what it is that needs doing. The fact that we pray at all is an affirmation that we believe in his power. But ironically, many times the very same prayer is a mute admission that we do not trust his wisdom. Even as we call on him to freely confess our powerlessness, we should also be confessing that we are about as wise as we are strong—and that the truth is we could use some help with the script too.

Jesus found the absolutes of his life in the will of the Father. And he tells us that we must do the same. When the disciples asked him to teach them how to pray, he gave them a marvelously simple model. Evelyn Underhill wrote about this prayer that we have said it and sung it so often that ". . . we are no longer conscious of its mysterious beauty and easily assume that we have long ago exhausted its inexhaustible significance."[9] One of its deep meanings is the guidance it gives us in centering our lives around the Eternal Source of purpose.

In the prayer he taught us it is evident that Jesus recognized our frailty and our weakness. He knew that all too often the reason we would be on our knees in prayer anyway would be because our needs would drive us there. He taught us that it is all right to come to the Father with the requests that have coiled themselves around the requisites and necessities of our daily living.

The assurance given in this prayer model is that the Father knows and cares and is abundantly able to bring about the answers. It is right, then, to pray, "Give us this day our daily bread." Jesus understood the present. He had been both tired and hungry. He had been discouraged and under fire and stretched out. And he was telling us that the Father can take care of us and wants to do so.

Jesus also understood about our yesterdays. He knew of the guilts and the associations of our past and he taught us to pray, "Forgive us our trespasses as we forgive those who trespass against us." He had seen the clouds from days gone by on the faces of those who had come to him. He had heard the past in the longing of their hearts even when their words could not admit it. And in the Father, he is telling us, there is release and freedom and forgiveness from the ravaging memory and debilitating guilt of the past.

He knew, too, that the joy of the present is often destroyed by the specter of some future happening or calamity. He had seen how the anxiety and worry of what may happen tomorrow could plague today. He is telling us to confess our perplexity about our future to the Father—and that we should be praying, "Lead us not into temptation but deliver us from evil." The God who can heal the past and provide for the present is also a God who knows the future.

So Jesus is telling us to bring all our needs and hopes to the Father when we pray. There is nothing that concerns us that does not also concern the Father. We do not have to wonder if he is interested in us or in the needs and necessities of our lives. Jesus assures us that he is interested.

It has been noted that when we are praying out of our present need for daily bread we are praying to God the Father, our Creator and Sustainer. When our petition is for forgiveness for our past we are praying to God the Son, our Redeemer and our Savior. And our prayers for the concerns of the future are prayers to God the Spirit, our Comforter and our Guide. So there is this deep and lovely sense in which Jesus is telling us to bring all there is of us—past, present and future—to all there is of God—Father, Son and Holy Spirit. He is telling us that in him there is to be found hope and help for the whole spectrum of life's needs.

Jesus is also making a deeper point here. He is telling us that we are not to begin our prayers from within the context of our own neediness. Our prayers, the deep outcries of our being, must grow out of the context of the wholeness of our eternal God. We are to forget, at least as we begin our prayers, our circumstances and our situations. We are to place our petitions within the bountifulness of the full particulars of God. Our first words in prayer are to be, "Our Father, who is in heaven, hallowed be your name, your kingdom come, your will be done on earth as it is in heaven."

Will Campbell, the Baptist preacher, philosopher, and writer, puts it this way: "With just ten words—'Our Father, who art in heaven, hallowed be thy name.'—Jesus had given . . . a theology, the only theology possible. A theology of the absolute sovereignty of God. And even 'absolute sovereignty' are insufficient words for the wordless One. Two thousand years, thousands more books and millions upon millions of words later the theology survives, and is all we can affirm about the Father with categorical certainty: God is God is God is God is God is God and then a period."[10]

Jesus was trying to teach us that the Father is the beginning from which all our lives must move and flow. He is the source out of which all the rest springs. Thus, our beginnings are anchored in his ancient purposes which grip us with their resolute steadfastness.

But Jesus is also telling us that the purposes of our prayers and our lives must also find their fruition in the Father. We are to remember that his is "the kingdom and the power and glory forever." Not only do we have a God who has gone before, but he is also the God who comes after. Thus, our endings are to become as secure and unchanging as our beginnings.

Our living, then, which is the fleshing out of our prayers, is to be securely fastened to the eternities both before and after us. Our prayers are to be a bridge over a world that is "transient and passing" into a "life that is eternal." The reference point is the deep purpose of God. He is the One who writes the script. He and he alone is the plot.

One of the things the calling voice of God is always bringing to us is a deep, undergirding, unchanging purpose. This alone can bring continuity to what we are and what we do. Our purposes are temporal and always changing. The desires which seem to motivate us and occupy the great share of our time and energy for a decade or two or three suddenly become unimportant as we enter a new season of our lives. There are times when the need is for bigger houses and bigger rooms. All of these larger spaces will require more and more stuff to fill them. The day will come when the children have moved away and we will be moving into a smaller place—and we will wonder how we are going to get rid of enough stuff to be able to squeeze into our new quarters. And if our lives are controlled by the needs or wants of a given day or decade we will always be disappointed in our quest for meaning and fulfillment. For permanence is not one of the attributes of our living.

Still we have an almost fatal affair with the temporal. At least, our preoccupation and attachment to things which are passing is almost an obsession with us. Looking again in my office there are two matters on the antique table that I use as my desk to which I presently am giving diligent attention. They will serve as proof to you that I am familiar with what I am writing about.

One is a set of papers that need to be signed which will complete my modest participation in a small real estate investment in Chattanooga, Tennessee. I am reading the enclosed prospectus which includes maps, pictures, legal descriptions and full financial information, including some predicted, but not promised, returns.

The other matter is the consideration of the proper promotion and advertising of a book I had written. I would like to do the things which will best insure its sale. This is no small matter to a writer. Somehow the simple sharing of some ideas with others on a printed page has a tendency to get deeply entangled with royalty rates, being well-known, invitations to speak, financial rewards and plain old-fashioned ego.

I feel it is important to me at this particular juncture of my life to make some careful investments both for the present and for the future well-being of my family. And having chosen, or perhaps being "chosen" to be a writer, it is also my responsibility to wisely propagate my books—for the next years of my life. It seems to follow that if you believe in what you are trying to communicate, you must also be diligent in enlarging the audience to whom you wish to pass along your thoughts.

Thus both of the issues for the day can be enobled by entitling them "stewardship" and "self-fulfillment." But, in truth, they are both parts of an order that is passing away. And I must be reminded that the real issue of permanence for me will not be determined by the success or failure of either or both of these matters. Rather, it will come as I know and relate myself to him "who was from the beginning" and who "abides forever."

Before there was an apartment complex in Chattanooga, before there was a Chattanooga or a Tennessee, or a United States, or a new world, or for that matter, an old world either—he was. And before there were books, or machines to print them on, or words to express thoughts or letters to form words—he was.

When my two-tenths of an apartment complex has either fallen down in decay or been pushed over by a bulldozer—he will still be. When my books have been discontinued by the publisher (perish the thought) and the last copy has finally disintegrated in somebody's attic (probably mine)—he will *still* be.

The meaning, the continuity, the rhyme, the reason, the plot, the purpose for us all are to be found in him and him alone. And that purpose is always calling us "to be conformed to the likeness of his Son."

4

The Language of
Religion Is Experience

" . . . in all things God works for the good of those who love him, who have been called according to his purpose."

ROMANS 8:28

And I said to the man who stood at the gate of the year: Give me a light that I may tread safely into the unknown. And he replied: Go out into the darkness and put thine hand into the hand of God. That shall be to thee better than light and safer than a known way.

M. L. HASKINS[1]

4
The Language of Religion
Is Experience

My mother, who brought up five children, recently wrote in her memoirs that I was "the only baby she raised who had none of the normal baby ailments." She reported that I "ate what I was fed, digested it, slept well, and was generally happy and a delight." Someone has since pointed out that I was either resting up to be sick from then on, or else I was playing some kind of monstrous trick on my parents—not to mention myself. My dad, who is the family historian, recently said that as far as he was able to determine, I was certainly among the leading contenders for being the sickest of the clan in at least seven or eight generations.

By the time I was four, my brother John was beginning to bring home from school all of the common childhood illnesses. In one year alone he spread measles, chicken pox and mumps through our household. Early on I showed a marked talent for getting sick as soon as the two of them, John and the disease, came in the door. Generally, I was not one to mess around with a mild case either.

When I was six years old or so I came down with severe asthma. This new ability to develop my own diseases marked a turning point in my life. No longer would I have to wait for someone to bring them to me. Ever since that time I have shown a remarkable propensity to come up with illnesses and maladies that are new to the family.

Bronchial asthma is among the most serious of childhood diseases and afflictions. It is baffling and capricious and unlike other illnesses such as scarlet fever or getting your tonsils taken out. You do not just get over it. One never seems to know when another attack is to be forthcoming.

For reasons unknown, asthma is usually a disease of the night, often occurring in the wee hours of the morning. It begins with a tightening of the chest and a dry cough. Breathing becomes more and more difficult until one is panting for air. In fact, the Greek word for asthma is "panting." This is accompanied by a deep wheezing and one is forced to sit up in bed, battling, struggling, fighting for breath with elbows propped on knees, shoulders hunched high and head thrown back literally gasping for air. It is a terrifying experience for a small boy—and I suspect it must have been equally terrifying for my young parents.[2]

Mom and Dad would come to me in the middle of the night with the usual treatments. There was the Asthma Nefrin nebulizer with the squeeze bulb that was good at dropping off and rolling under the bed. And there was a greenish powder called Asthmador which you burned in a jar lid so you could inhale the smoke. I would pile it up like a tiny mountain and light it in one spot and watch the flaming sparks spread like a forest fire until it was blackened all over. Hopefully, the rising smoke allowed me enough breath to lie down again and go back to sleep. Asthmador also came in cigarettes and as a mixture for pipe smoking, but, of course, I only read about these forms of evil on the side of the can.

On cold winter nights when an attack would come and I would be unable to breathe lying down, Dad would build a fire in the fireplace and tuck the covers around me in his big, easy chair. Mom would read to me until I would finally fall asleep again. Sometimes, if the nebulizer or the smoke wouldn't work, they would bundle me up and take me over to Dr. Elliott's house on Eastdale Avenue for a shot of adrenaline.

Between attacks there were trips to all kinds of doctors and specialists with numerous tests to try to determine what was the cause. It was apparent that the fall of the year was the most difficult season for me and that ragweed and other things in the air would give me attacks. I spent many weeks out of school and the home-bound teacher would come to me. Sometimes my mother would take me to North Carolina to see if the mountain air would help. Sometimes we would go to Florida or the Alabama coast to see if the sea air was any freer of the pollens that provoked the attacks. But usually something—dust, pollen, damp night air, changes in temperature, cat fur, dog hair, feather pillows, being at home, being away from home, or some culprit unknown to us—managed to continue to disrupt my life by provoking asthma to "attack" me.

Even when I was feeling well enough to go to school, there were many notes sent along to everybody about how to "take care of Bob." Of course, I was told always to keep my head covered, my sweater on and my feet dry. Once I remember it started snowing one afternoon while we were in school. The class could hardly wait for the bell to ring so we could get out into the big, moist snowflakes that were already beginning to cover the ground. There was a knock on the seventh grade classroom door and I saw a mother's hand pass a pair of galoshes through the crack in the doorway to the teacher. Being especially susceptible to such protection, I remember thinking how embarrassed some poor kid was going to be. And I can remember even clearer the feeling when Mrs. McDaniel turned to the class and said, "Bob Benson, come get your galoshes."

As you might well imagine, as a father now, I have a much deeper appreciation for my parents' investment in midnight vigils and trips to anywhere there might be help and galoshes when it began to snow during the school day.

Listening to the Processes

I don't always know what to say about my illnesses. As much of the time as we can at our house, we try to laugh about them. Just the other morning Peg remarked that she had a cold and I responded, "I do too." She accused me of trying to have everything she did. So we decided to divide the diseases. She would have all the minor ones and I would have all the major stuff—the things that really bring out people's sympathy and flowers and cookies and cards. In the case of a brand new disease, I am to get the first option until we find out whether it is going to be major or not.

But then again I don't know what to say about my wellnesses, either. As surely as I do not understand why I so often have been the one to get sick, neither do I understand why I am the one who has so often gotten well from so many things. But I do believe that something has grown out of both experiences over the years that has enriched the soil into which my faith has sunk its roots.

There was some kind of lesson learned, however faint it might have been when I was younger. Maybe it was about vulnerability. To be sure, there were mornings when it was nice in a way to be staying home as John and Laura were getting ready for school. But there were other times when I could not help but wonder why I wasn't as sturdy as Bill Hunt or Roland Downing or Mack Parsons who always seemed ready to play in the woods and along the creek that flowed through our back yard.

Early on, there was a dimly increasing awareness that all was not as it was purported to be. That even though it seemed that most of life's lessons had to do with oneself—self-control, self-development, self-assertiveness, self-preservation—maybe there was something truer to be learned. It was simple on the surface. One only had to learn to talk, walk, dress, read, write, add, subtract, multiply, divide, ride a bicycle, drive a car, acquaint oneself with some important, but never again to be used, facts—such as Boise is the capital of Idaho and water is one part hydrogen and two parts oxygen. One had to learn to make choices and to make waves and to make a living—and then came the rewards: self-confidence, self-support, self-reliance. Completedness.

It is a strong theory but it doesn't always test out well when as a kid you wake up in the middle of the night unable to catch your breath. Or later on, in a sort of a mid-life course correction, when a doctor tells you this particular lump is malignant and must be removed. One does not particularly become a theologian at seven (or at forty-two, either), but there has always seemed to be the sound of other meanings coming forth from somewhere back there—a sound that quietly but firmly pointed out that faith would have to find its refuge outside of self. That sound gently but resolutely confirmed that there was One who could gather up the circumstances of our days and use them to his purposes and to our good.

It is partially, at least, from this perspective of illness and wellness that I so strongly see and believe this fact: one can come to know that God is infinitely willing and abundantly able to bring good out of the processes of our lives. Perhaps this is also where I have begun to learn to hear the calling voice of God in the happenings and events of life.

There is an expression we frequently use that probably means more than we originally intended. When people first give their hearts to Christ we say they have made a *profession of faith*. They are saying that they believe (even to the point of committing their lives) the promises of God as given to us in his Son Jesus Christ our Lord. They are professing to believe in his forgiveness, his steadfastness, his love, his companionship, his will, and his victory over evil.

It is unfortunate that new believers are often more earnest and zealous in giving testimony to their newfound faith than many of us who have been "in the way" for a long time. Of course, everything these "professers" are saying is true. What the sophomore baritone of the quartet on tour from the denominational college is saying about the "everlasting" faithfulness of God is certainly true. But from the perspective of his experience he just does not know it yet. The promises of God may be claimed, they may be quoted, they may be *professed*. But it takes the processes of a lifetime to *possess* them.

The title of Dorothee Soelle's book, *Death by Bread Alone*, caught my attention in a bookstore one afternoon. I am indebted to her for the phrase, "the language of religion is experience" as well as new insight into the moving thought behind it. In the book she writes about a deep experience she had gone through. It was a very trying time in her life which she could only describe as "almost like dying":

I must have reached the middle of the tunnel of despair at that point. I had not the faintest idea what that theological term "grace" meant because it had absolutely nothing to do with the reality of my life. And yet "God" had spoken that word to me. . . . Gradually, it began to dawn on me that people who believe limp somewhat, as Jacob limped after wrestling with God on the shore of the Jabbok. All of them died at one time or another. We cannot wish such a death upon another, nor can we spare another from experiencing it by giving some kind of instruction. The experience of faith can be no more vicarious than the pleasure of physical love. The experience of the sufficiency of grace for life, and the experience that nothing—not even our own death—can separate us from the love of God, are experiences we can recognize only after the fact. Such experiences are not written down and incorporated in drawings and plans which we can examine and check during the course of construction.[3]

Perhaps no writer in the New Testament is clearer about the relationship of experience to faith than John. In the prologue to the Gospel that bears his name he proclaims, "In the beginning was the Word, and the Word was with God, and the Word was God. He was with God in the beginning" (1:1). Then he makes this remarkable announcement and claim, "The Word became flesh and lived for a while among us. We have seen his glory . . ." (v. 14).

John never forgot what he had seen. Over a half a century later he sent a pastoral letter to the various churches under his charge. In what has been called by some "a loving and anxious sermon," he wrote these words: "That which was from the beginning, which we have heard, which we have seen with our eyes, which we have looked at and our hands have touched— this we proclaim concerning the Word of life" (1 John 1:1).

I am aware that "the language of religion is experience" in graphic ways. It is painfully obvious to me that I am bounded in my words by the things I have experienced in God. Always I pray before addressing an audience that my words will reveal what God has come to mean in my life. But I must also acknowledge in prayer and contrition that I have not hungered enough for him, or confessed enough to him, or lived long enough in him to begin to know many of the things he would have me know. I can say the things I do know about him with deepest conviction and love. But I am always aware of this so-bering thought—the things I know best about him are things I have learned through the processes of day-to-day living. So I shouldn't have to fear "tomorrow."

The processes of life are one of the ways we come to know him as we should. We start out with a "profession of faith." It is not that what we are saying is not true—his promises are defi-nitely real. But we do not *own* these beliefs yet because we have not bought them with the experiences of our journey. Someday we will. Someday they will be uniquely ours, to possess and to share.

I remember when I first started working in my father's music company in Nashville. One afternoon Dad took me up to the ninth floor of the old Third National Bank Building to meet Mr. Louis Farrell. Mr. Louis, as I call him, had been the attorney for the Benson companies for a number of years. Just keeping up with the Benson brothers and their sons and daughters and all the complications of a family business must have taken a good bit of wisdom at times. He is, as he says, a tough old bird. And it must have taken somebody pretty tough to straighten out or extricate some temporarily misguided member of the clan at times. Through it all he managed to remain both our attorney and a friend of the family.

Recently I learned that Mr. Louis had been in the hospital for surgery. Before I found out about it he was already at home recuperating. One afternoon I stopped by his house to see how he was getting along. He was sitting out in the backyard enjoy-ing the sunshine and I joined him for a visit. It was nice to be talking without the legal meter running, and I learned some things about him that I had never known. He had not always been in that office in the bank building. At one time he had been a little boy. He had brothers and sisters and had gone to grammar school and grown up just like the rest of us. He had skinned his knees and ridden bicycles and played ball and courted the girls. I guess I should have suspected that he had not been born an attorney at the corner of Fourth Avenue and Church Street.

After we had visited awhile he said to me, "Bob, I don't want to bore you or keep you too long, but I do want to tell you something that happened to me during this illness." I could sense that he was getting ready to tell me something that had touched him deeply.

"Down across the years," he began, "I have taught a men's Bible class at the church. We used many different books from both the Old and New Testaments, but I guess my favorite place has always been the Gospel of John. I have returned to it time and again. One of the things that I always seemed to see so clearly was John's teaching about eternal life—life as it is brought to us in Christ Jesus. And I taught, as I think John wrote, that when we come to Christ we come into eternal life. Right then. It is not a life that comes to us when this one is over. It is in us and we are in it now.

"When I learned I was going to have surgery I was not really afraid. I had to wait a week for our family surgeon to return from vacation and I went through the whole process—waiting, preparation, surgery, recovery room, recuperation—and all without ever being even the least bit apprehensive. I was gripped by a deep sense of serenity and peace. I found that I really believed what I had been teaching all these years. I was already living eternal life, and where I lived it was not really all that important."

There was peace in his eyes and satisfaction in his voice. I knew he had come to terms with himself. And one of those terms was faith. What had been a lifelong profession of his now belonged to him. It was his possession. He knew that what he had said he *believed* was true really *was* true. And his faith belonged to him.

Experience only comes as we go through the processes. We can only come to "know" about God's providential care in the living out of our lives. And it is this knowledge of him which comes in the processes of life and of death that is referred to in Romans 8:28:" . . . "in all things God works for the good of those who love him, who have been called according to his purpose."

Believing All They Say

Over and over I hear people affirm God's unfailing power to bring good from the circumstances of life. Sometimes in retreat prayertimes, I will ask the people to envision a blank sheet of paper with a horizontal line across the middle. Then, giving them time for reflection, I ask them to remember the good things that have happened to them over the years—to think about them and rejoice over them. And I have them "write" those things one by one on the paper above the line. (I confess that I often "watch and pray" so that I may enjoy the looks of peace and pleasure on the faces in front of me.)

Then, to help them get a truer perspective of how God works in their lives, I also suggest they recall the evil things that have come to them as well—the dark, deep, troublesome times that threatened to engulf their souls. I ask them to "list" those below the line. And I watch the expressions of pain move across their faces as they recall things that had swept in on them with devastating suddenness and fury. I try to close these prayertimes by reminding the audience that the whole paper can be committed to him. He is God of the list on the top and God of the list on the bottom.

A very interesting thing always happens afterward. Sometimes just one person and sometimes several people will find me afterward just to talk. The places may vary, but the conversation is always the same: "You know when we were listing those things on the paper in prayer . . . and we put that stuff above and below the line. There were some things that, for the life of me, I didn't know where to put. Even now I am not sure. Some of those things are so evil it would seem their place would be a foregone conclusion. The day they happened I knew, all right. The bottom of the bottom wasn't low enough. I did not know whether I would make it or not. I thought I was going to die. But now, looking back, I'm not so sure. Some of them seem to be creeping over the line."

In their eyes there usually is a depth that reveals a mixture of both joy and sorrow, both peace and pain. Their brows are often furrowed and many times their hair is gray. But they say to me, "I guess I have to write it above the line." Even out of the direst circumstances his call to us can be heard.

More and more it seems that those of us who make up retreats are a microcosm of society in general. One has only to show a little bit of openness and willingness to listen to be allowed into the worlds of hurt reflecting all of the ills of society. For we are, or carry the burdens of, the sick, the deranged, the illegitimate, the elderly, the divorced, the poor, the unloved, and the unwanted. We are all there. Almost anything that has happened anywhere has happened at some time to one of us.

I listen to people and my heart breaks for them. Sometimes I think I would like to put my arms around them and promise them I will personally see that nothing else bad ever happens to them again. But I cannot even protect my own from the hurts of life. There are only about three things I know to say to them. The first is that I will pray for them.

Sometimes I think we just say we will pray for someone because there doesn't seem to be anything which we consider practical or helpful we can do—something like sit with the children or cook supper or run some errands. So we say, "I'll pray for you." I am coming to believe that there is nothing more important that we can do for anyone than to pray for them. I confess to them that I am not so good at it, but I do have time and I will pray for them—and for their son, or daughter, or estranged husband, or diseased body, or perplexing situation.

I have found that offering to pray for someone often leads me to ask if there is anything else I can do. For we cannot let them into our hearts alone. Prayer is not an escape from the pain and reality of the world; rather it is a clearer, more compelling awareness of it. And we are led to some other way in which we may be of help.

The other thing that I always want to do is to try to impart this truth—God is able to work in the darkest, direst set of circumstances. Many times, in the light of the story just told me, it seems impertinent or even irreverent to suggest it. Still, on the basis of the gospel, and on the basis of my own experiences up to this point in my life, I want to tell those people that I believe God will turn their sorrows into joy.

I know there are tragic and terrible things which befall people. There are wrongs that can never be righted again—events and misfortunes that are still as unfair and as bewildering years later as they were the dark night they occurred. And even though it seems almost a sacrilege to say it to the broken, wounded person who stands weeping before me, I always find myself telling them, "Someday you will sing about this very sorrow."

We may lay claim to the promises of God in a moment of profession. We may rest on them. We may trust them implicitly. We may live in accordance with the precepts and admonitions. We may read and memorize the words of Jesus and be certain that they are true. We may have no doubt that God will be with us always because he has promised that he would. But somewhere on the journey, pain or sickness or sorrow will overwhelm us like a flood. And we will realize that we are not alone. Then the promise will be ours. Our faith will belong to us.

Knowing his presence, knowing that he is indeed who he says he is, and knowing that he can do what he claims he can do become the truths that form his message to us. That message tells us "in all things" he is working for our good. And the joy of "knowing him" is the joy that transforms our sorrows.

I was in the music business for twenty years. In all that time I did not write one song. Only a time or two did I even help with one. Phil Johnson, talented young songwriter, producer and friend at the company, came into my office one morning and wanted me to listen to a new song he had written. It was to be recorded that very afternoon. It was such a lovely idea for a song that I suggested that he hold it for awhile—to give it time to grow and come to full blossom in his heart and mind. He was gracious enough to accept my suggestion and even asked if I would like to work on it with him. As I recall I wrote a verse and helped some on the chorus. I still believe the things we wrote are true.

> He never said you'd only see sunshine,
>   He never said there'd be no rain.
> He only promised a heart full of singing
>   About the very things that once brought pain.
>
> Give them all, give them all,
>   Give them all to Jesus,
> Shattered dreams, wounded hearts,
>   and broken toys;
> Give them all, give them all,
>   Give them all to Jesus,
> And he will turn your sorrows into joys.[4]

I saw a little lady recently who was perfectly demonstrating this matter of sorrow and joy. I was in Ohio to speak, and before the service I was taken out to dinner by the pastor of the church and his wife. We were old college and seminary friends, so it was a special evening for me. As we were being shown to our table they waved to someone across the room. When we were seated they told me the little old lady they had waved to was a member of their church. I looked at her, sitting there alone in the booth, dressed in what appeared to be her Sunday best. It was obvious she was having the deluxe dinner—salad, baked potato, roast beef, hot rolls.

As we went to the salad bar ourselves we all spoke and she told us she was having a celebration. Gene and I went back to the table with our salads but Francis sat down beside her for a moment to ask her what she was celebrating. Now, of course, Gene and I are much too spiritual to eat without saying grace, and much too gentlemanly to pray without Francis. So we both were surreptitiously nibbling croutons as we waited.

When she came her eyes were glistening with tears. She told us the beautiful story she had just heard. The little lady had first asked her, "Did you know my husband died not long ago?"

And Francis said, "Yes, I knew. I was at the funeral when my husband preached."

"Well, I had been so blue and so despondent," she continued, "I hardly cared if I lived myself. The other night, the Lord told me I couldn't keep on like I was doing. I couldn't stay buried in my grief. I had to cheer up, and smile, and begin to get out of the house some. My reply to him was, 'I can't, Lord. I'm all alone.'

"And then the Lord said, 'But you still have me.'

"And I am here tonight eating this meal in glad celebration that it is true. I still have him."

I looked across at this solitary celebrant again. There was a radiance about her that could not have come from the late afternoon sunlight streaming in the window above her. The light in her eyes came from deep within her heart in glad affirmation that the gentle, comforting, calling voice of God can be heard in even the deepest valleys of our lives.

Listen to all that life has to say to you. He calls you from the processes.

5

When Something
Holy Happens

"God . . . has called you into fellowship with
his Son Jesus Christ our Lord . . . ."

1 CORINTHIANS 1:9

*To pray is to take notice of the wonder, to regain a sense of the mystery that
animates all things, the divine margin in all attainments. Prayer is our
humble answer to the inconceivable surprise of living. It is all we can offer in
return for the mystery by which we live.*

RABBI ABRAHAM JOSHUA HESCHEL[1]

5
When Something Holy Happens

I am a believer in moments.

In early November last year, Peg and I were taking a trip together, and while we were traveling along, we worked out our budget for Christmas. We listed all those to whom we wanted to give presents and how much we thought we could spend for them. We could have done a little better all the way around, I guess, but we also decided to spend some money on moments.

We put aside some money for groceries, so we could have some friends over. We set aside money to take the boys and their dates to see Dickens' great classic, "A Christmas Carol," which was going to be staged downtown at the Tennessee Performing Arts Center. For the night when Leigh came in from college, we planned a big evening out, all dressed up for dinner in the Hermitage Hotel Dining Room. And there was money designated to decorate the house with candles and wreaths and angels and ribbons and bells and greenery and goodwill.

Of course, we have been around long enough to know that money won't necessarily buy a moment. Indeed, moments can't be purchased. You've been places, haven't you, where they said that something was going to happen and you paid your money and went and nothing did happen? But we were determined to decorate the walls, dim the lights, light the candles, ring the bells, and sing the carols so that if a moment decided it wanted to happen to us, or among us, it would sure know it was welcome.

I'm not sure that I even know how to describe a moment when it comes. (Most of the time they come unexpectedly anyway.) I'm not sure I know how to define "it" when it happens. But I know it when it does.

Our family does have a way of rating experiences together. One of the gauges of our pleasure was discovered when someone noticed that Peggy snorted when she was really tickled at something. Since that time, the highest rating a joke can get at our house is a three-snorter. They may come when we are all laughing or teasing—or they have been known to slip in along with someone's illness or struggle. The way we seem to recognize a moment at our house is that it is usually accompanied by lumps in our throats and tears in our eyes. And all of a sudden, we are standing there in the midst of a moment.

On Christmas Eve the larger family gathered at our house to eat dinner and exchange gifts. Wally and Jean, Bo and Peggy's parents, Bo, Robert, Jetta and grandson Robert, Leigh, Tom, Patrick, Peg and I made up the crowd. The only empty places in this annual gathering were because Mike, Gwen, and Katie were in Colorado. It was Mike's first Christmas as a pastor and so they were not home for the holidays. (I am not as sure as I used to be that the pastor always has to be at his church for Christmas.) Sometimes a dash of sadness hastens the coming of a moment.

When the food was ready and it was time to eat we went into the living room. We stood in a circle around the *creche.* A solitary candle flickered light across the manger and the baby. With our arms around each other we sang:

> . . . O come let us adore him,
> O come let us adore him,
> Christ the Lord.

Although I was not the ranking grandfather that night I wanted to lead in prayer. I bowed my head and, as best I could, I began to lift our thankfulness and praise for all that had come to us because he had come into the world in a manger—for family, for belonging, for grandparents and for grandchildren. And Robert added, "and brothers and sisters." The amen was pronounced and as we started for the dining room it was easy enough to see, even through blurry eyes, that we had just experienced a moment.

There was dinner with all the trimmings—macaroni and cheese like only Grandmother Siler can make, Bo's green beans and her squash casserole, Jetta's pies and cheesecake, and Peg's turkey and dressing and rolls. When we all had eaten far more than we should have, and the kitchen was clean, and the dishes were put away, we went into the den by the fire and took our places to open the piles of presents beneath the tree. There were "oohs" and "ahhs" and "thank yous" and hugs and squeals of surprise and delight as we opened the things we had bought and made for each other. I really think that those who had made gifts were the happiest of all, for they had given so much of themselves. Gwen's stuffed geese and her lacy pillows and Leigh's handpainted stationery with the paint still wet, to name a few, were gifts that drew loud praise.

Finally, the gifts were all opened and the wrapping paper and ribbon had been cleaned up. Peg suggested I read Truman Capote's *A Christmas Memory* to them all. I was happy to oblige. In fact I was just wishing someone would ask me. Fred Bock had given me the little book some weeks before and I had read it in some of the places I had spoken during the Christmas season. So I reached under my chair and pulled it out and began before the offer was withdrawn.

It is a beautiful, moving story about a Christmas when Truman was seven and living with his Aunt Sook who was in her sixties. It is a long-ago moment from his life made all the more poignant when you consider the strange directions in which he was finally taken by his fame and riches. His parents were divorced and neither wanted little Truman. So he was sent to live with some elderly relatives, and this old aunt was his best friend and companion. By the time I got to Christmas Day, when he and the old lady were flying the kites they had made for each other, our den was laden with warmth and feeling. They had made the kites because they had spent all their money making and mailing fruitcakes to others. I read things she said to him, "I've always thought a body would have to be sick and dying before they saw the Lord. And I imagined that when he came it would be like looking at the Baptist window: pretty as colored glass with the sun pouring through, such a shine you don't know it's getting dark. And it's been a comfort to think of that shine taking away all the spooky feeling. But I'll wager it never happens. I'll wager at the very end a body realizes the Lord has already shown himself. That things as they are"—her hand circles in a gesture that gathers clouds and kites and grass and Queenie pawing earth over her bone—"just what they've always been, was seeing him. As for me, I could leave the world with today in my eyes."[2] It was quiet enough to hear the tears gently falling from our cheeks onto our Christmas finery. Sometimes it seems moments must travel in pairs.

Evenings like that come and go all too quickly. Too soon it was time for coats and hats and gloves and carrying-out-to-the-cars and then farewells. We were all standing in the kitchen saying our last good-byes, when Peg saw something on the counter top some friends had sent to us a few weeks before. It was an Erma Bombeck column entitled *One of These Days*. It was about some moments that had crystalized in her life. Peg began to read Erma's words: "One of these days you'll shout, 'Why don't you kids grow up and act your age?' And they will." She ends, "Only a voice crying, 'Why don't you grow up?' And the silence echoing, 'I did.' "[3] There was enough stuff in the middle about no more nights in a vaporizer tent and no more carpools and PTA and wet-knotted shoestrings and tight boots to cause all four generations in my kitchen to stand unabashedly touched.

And we all exclaimed almost together, "What a Christmas celebration—it has been a three-sniffler." (Maybe that's not a record, but it's a good average.)

The socks will wear out and the ties will get spots on them and the sweaters will stretch out of shape. But the moments are tucked away in our memories for all time and will only improve with age. They will be brighter and happier every time we take them out to enjoy and celebrate.

I am a believer in moments.

The Sacrament of Life

Frederick Buechner says that "a sacrament is when something holy happens." He goes on to explain that it is actually where we notice that something holy is happening. And he says, "If we weren't blind as bats we might see that life itself is sacramental."[4] When God calls us "into fellowship with his Son Jesus Christ our Lord," I hear him inviting us to the awareness of the sweetness and mystery of life itself.

The ancient prayer ending that comes down to us," . . . through Jesus Christ our Lord. Amen," is more than a ritual. It is more than a formality or a formula. It is the true and significant cornerstone of our praying and our living. Life is to be found through him, in fellowship with him.

It seems that this was at least partly what Paul was hearing, too. He writes ". . . of his grace given you in Christ Jesus . . . in him you have been enriched in every way, . . . Therefore you do not lack any spiritual gift. . . . He will keep you strong to the end . . . you will be blameless . . . ." (1 Cor. 1:4–8). All of these things come to us in Christ Jesus. They are bestowed on us as we answer the call into fellowship with him. He is the place where the holy shines through. He is the point through which the life of God flows into us and into our actions. He breathes the breath of life into us and into our everydays. He is the One who puts substance into the forms of our living. He is the very substance of life itself. But we are so often content with just the form.

I think it is fair to say that we Americans have a great preoccupation with the form, and only make mild protests for the substance of life itself. This is apparent from the most casual observations about our society.

Forms without Substance

My travels to retreats and conferences have taken me to nearly every section of the country, and I am constantly amazed with the diversity of this great land. Almost every part has something which gives the region a distinctiveness. It seems that God has done something wonderfully different around almost every curve and just over every hill.

You cannot make the same claim for what we humans wreak on the landscape. There is an ever-expanding sameness about what has been built up at the intersections and the crossroads of America. Perhaps Exit 78 on Interstate 30 in Arkansas is as good a place as any to illustrate. Located roughly halfway between Little Rock and Texarkana, it is everything the familiar sign, "Gas, Food, and Lodging" proclaims. Everything is crowded here into a half mile strip along U.S. Highway 67 and State Route 7. Standing in a row with their signs raised to the sky they beckon to the weary traveler. Anywhere, USA. *Exxon, McDonalds* (50 Billion Sold), *Shell, Conoco, Gulf, Holiday Inn* ("Welcome Kiwanis"), a couple of local entries—*Pig Pit Barbecue, Caddos Grocery and Live Bait*—and my destination, *Continental Motor Inn* beckoning "Welcome Nazarenes" and "Cable TV."

As I drove down the exit ramp, it was very easy for me to feel that I had been here before. If I had any feelings of strangeness at all, they were quickly dispelled when I lugged my suitcase and boxes of books into the familiar surroundings of Room 111 here in this member of the World's Largest Lodging Chain. The use of the word "chain" seemed unfortunate to me, since I was already longing to be home.

Somewhere in the higher councils of motel management it must have been foreordained that henceforth all motel rooms contain at least one bed, one tv, one table (preferably octagonally shaped and made out of oak), two flanking chairs, one dresser with a counter smartly attached for your suitcase, two bars of soap, two bath towels, two washcloths, two plastic cups wrapped for your sanitary drinking, one splashy set of matching drapes and bedspread, and two early American prints on the wall. All of this luxury is made complete with the name of the establishment stamped on ashtrays and matches, and it is hard to think of anything else one might need.

The *McDonalds* across the highway was not a disappointment, either, for it, too, had the familiar, comfortable feel of being planned at corporate headquarters. The boxes, the buns, the uniforms—they all made me feel like I had never left home. It's not hard to bump into the American dream these days, even at Exit 78.

Once in awhile, though, it does seem to me that the dream has worn a little thin here and there. Most of the dreamers these days seem to be waiting for someone else to do something that can be duplicated, imitated, copied, franchised, and reproduced in living plastic, preferably for a profit. If the form can be copied skillfully enough, probably no one will even notice there is a decided lack of substance. If it looks like a motel, that must be what is—and if it is shaped like a hamburger, it must be one.

Some time ago in Nashville a group of enterprising investors opened a "pilot model" for a new chain of fast food stores, as they call them in the trade. The speciality was to be steak and biscuits. The idea was good enough, although certainly not new. A well-known personality, who for some reason was supposed to immediately remind us all of steak and biscuits, lent his name to be used for an appropriate fee. There was ample capital and the stores were bright and cheery. There were only two minor problems. The first was that the steak was bad. The second was that the biscuits were worse. It was like the old saying, "If we had some bacon we would have bacon and eggs, if we had some eggs." Hooray for Nashvillians. Enough of us managed to stay away to get him to go away. The rest of America owes us a heartfelt thanks for nipping this franchise in the bud.

I don't mean to seem unduly hard on the eating and lodging habits of the American public. My concern about the balance between substance and form is deeper than Gas, Food, and Lodging. My real lament is that sooner or later what is happening to us in society begins to make itself felt in the church as well. The influence of mass economy—standard operating procedures, checklists, symbols, signs, style, slogans, contests, and other activities—begin to lead the church subtly away from being a place of substance. The danger is that it then takes its place at the intersection with all the other forms of what we call American life. And one steeple, eighty-nine pews, a six-person staff, two parking lots, four used buses and fourteen special events for every member of the family to do four nights a week may or may not be a church.

A couple of springs ago, I was with the teens from our church on a retreat. That Sunday morning, we met in a country church for our service. The pastor let us in at an early hour so we could have the building to ourselves. I told those young people we were going to imagine we were having church just like they were having it back home. Who, and what, did we need to have church? They began to name ushers, organist, pastors and all the other people who are to be found in and around the church. Then a member of the group took the place of each one named.

When we had finished "populating" the church, we reversed the procedure by asking who and what could we do away with and still be a church. One by one we all returned to our seats as they decided you could have church without ushers, without an organist, without a choir, and finally, they even let the pastor go. When we were all sitting back down we began to discuss who and what was really necessary to having church. Their answers finally led us to the conclusion that the church was a very simple gathering. It takes some believers, some nonbelievers whom the believers were trying to win, and the presence of Jesus. All the rest, they concluded, was just part of the *form* of the church.

The substance is people made alive with the presence of Christ. It is the presence of Christ that makes a group of people into a church. And all the rest of it is just form. But it seems to be commonly believed that the essence of the church is the number of activities undertaken.

I am on the mailing list of many churches from different parts of the country. And nobody can say that the church is not busy. Just reading two newsletters at random off my desk makes me glad I am on the retreat circuit. I do not think my health is good enough to be a regular attender at either of these churches. There were three picnics, four lunches, two brunches, two canoe trips, one splash bash, one softball makeup game, one ice cream dream, one volleyball tournament, trips to the State Fair, Chattanooga, Gatlinburg, Mammoth Cave, and the International Youth Convention, two baby showers, one call for basketball, three aerobics classes and an announcement (it seems more like a warning) that the bowling season would soon be upon us all. Needless to say, there were also board meetings, prayer meetings, committee meetings, youth meetings, senior citizens meetings, couples meetings, singles meetings, board meetings and district meetings. I am not trying to say that I think all of those activities are just form. But I do think it is fair to say this: it is going to take a whole lot of substance to make all of that form a redemptive part of the body of Christ.

Jesus Brings the Holy

There are ample signs that we are equally as form-conscious in our personal lives. We are a status-conscious, appearance-oriented generation wearing the labels of our clothes on the outside to prove to each other that we are somebody and that we belong. And it is into our franchised, plastic, instant, disposable, wash and wear, no down payment, planned obsolescence world of sham and surface shine that the calling of God comes. He wants to bring us to an authenticity and realness that can fill the days of our lives with rich meaning.

We all are aware of how some ordinary thing can become sacramental to us. Some simple pieces of cloth, stitched together in a special way, come to represent our love of liberty and home, and are thus worthy of our bared heads and our crossed hearts. A wilted dandelion somehow forever deserves a place tucked away in our Bible because it was delivered in the grubby fist of a four-year-old. In some way, these become magnetic symbols around which our feelings gather. One of the things I am hearing over and over again is that it is the desire and intent of Jesus to sacramentalize the commonplace—to bring the meaning and purpose that only his life can bring into the ordinary moments and places and happenings of our lives. Probably we are never far away from something which should be reminding us that we are never very far away from him.

This ability of his to make everything into a sacrament was evident from the very beginning of his life among us. Take the manger scene itself. At our house, we have a lovely set of wood carvings of the baby Jesus, Mary, Joseph, the angels and the shepherds. It also includes some sheep, lambs, horses, cows, calves, ponies, and even a sleeping rooster. Peg and I brought the set when we were browsing through some shops in New Orleans one fall. We had wanted a *creche* in our home for a long time, and we were taken with the beauty of these figures. Peg is really the decorator at our house, and she has a knack for displaying things at their best and making places look special. But she agreed to let me set up the manger scene the first season. I must have done a pretty good job because I am now the official manger-scene builder. She did request that I hone my skills on the sunporch that first year, but now the scene occupies the central place in our living room.

I have accumulated a box or two of materials that I use along with the carvings. There are some pieces of driftwood I picked up on our various vacations on the coast. I take them out of the box each year like old friends. I know each one of them for its special size and shape and smoothness. I wish that I could ask them questions and hear them answer back: "Where did you begin your journey? What kind of tree were you? What brought you crashing down? How did you get washed up on that lonely stretch of beach? Did you once hold up a little girl's swing or a boy's tree house? Were you part of a house or a boat or a packing box?" For I believe that everything has a story; it has been somewhere, and it is going somewhere.

I also have a collection of stones and rocks. I found them on trips, too—in fields and mountain streams and by country roads. They, too, I suspect, could tell me many things if I just knew how to listen to them. Annie Dillard wrote about a man in her neighborhood who spent all his spare time trying to teach a stone to talk. I think about him every year when I take my stones out of the box.

In early December, I get out all these manger things. With the stones, I make a rocky hillside, and with the wood, I build a barn and a stall. I carefully place the manger, the baby Jesus, Mary, Joseph, and all the rest of the figures (right down to the sleeping rooster) on the roof. Then I light the candle, sit down before this scene again, and try to imagine how this holy story could ever have happened at all.

Admittedly, I have gathered up the materials for this scene from lots of places. But always I am impressed to remember that everything needed to make this sacred tableau can be found in anybody's neighborhood. Sticks and stones, straw and foliage, dogs and cats, neighbors, and a virgin girl—all of them can be touched with the meaning that only Christ can bring: meaning that will obliterate the lines which separate the divine and the commonplace, meaning that changes a stall into a holy place, and a manger into an altar.

Men could only describe the things Jesus did as he walked among them as miracles. His mother took him to a wedding in the very first days of his ministry. She was embarrassed for her friends because the wine ran out and she turned to Jesus for help. There were six jars sitting beside the door. They were used to hold the water the Jews used to wash their feet and hands—to cleanse themselves ceremonially. They were empty, and Jesus asked the servants to fill them with water. Try to imagine their chagrin when he told them to draw out a pitcher of this bathwater and take it to the master of the feast. Try to imagine their surprise when the master tasted it and wondered why the bridegroom had saved the best wine until last. John said that this was the first of Christ's "miraculous signs."

Another day a blind man stood before him. Jesus knelt down and spit in the dust. With his finger he stirred the saliva into the dirt. Jesus took the mud, smeared it on the man's eyelids, and told him that if he would wash in the pool of Siloam, his eyes would be healed. The man did as he was told, and went back to his village seeing his home for the first time in his life.

This ability to transform the commonplace was even more evident in the events that surrounded Jesus' death. On the eve of his betrayal, Jesus and his disciples celebrated Passover in an upper room. He wanted it to be a sacramental meal—one they would always remember. So he blessed a crust of bread and a cup of wine and shared them with his disciples. From the two most common elements of every Palestinian meal he made his monument. Someone has written, " 'When you see alabaster gleaming in resplendent beauty, remember the body broken for you. In frankincense and myrrh illuminated by the fire of rubies, pledge the new covenant in my blood! Jesus did not say this, but why didn't he say something like that? Why not a costly memorial, something inaccessible and infinitely precious, that would best symbolize the inexpressible worth of the Son of Man?"[5]

The reason, of course, was that he wanted symbols within the reach of everyone. Nobody was so poor that they did not have bread and wine. The bread might have been as hard as a stone, and the wine might have been bitter and filled with dregs, but it would serve to refresh the body in that land of sparse wells. And both would have been on the table of even the poorest of peasants.

So a supper became a sacrament—a place where the holy life of God happened. Because of that meal we should burst into song. For it is saying to us as loudly as we will let it, "there is life in the touch of Jesus." Hans Küng reminds us "if the Church owes to baptism the fact that it is a Church and does not have to become a Church through its own pious works, it owes to the Lord's Supper the fact that it remains a Church, despite any falling away or failure."[6]

Thomas G. Pettepiece tells a lovely story about the bread and the wine in his book, *Visions of a World Hungry*. He tells of being in prison with some 10,000 other political prisoners. It was Easter Sunday and a score of Christians wanted to take communion, but there was neither bread nor wine available. He relates: "We have no bread, nor water to use instead of wine . . . but we will act as though we had. . . . I held out my empty hand to the first person on my right, and placed it over his open hand, and the same with the others. 'Take, eat, this is my body which is given for you; do this in remembrance of me.' Afterward, all of us raised our hands to our mouths, receiving the body of Christ in silence. 'Take, drink, this is the blood of Christ which was shed to seal the new covenant of God with men. Let us give thanks, sure that Christ is here with us, strengthening us'. . . . We gave thanks to God, and finally stood up and embraced each other."[7]

If he can take sticks, stones, straw, bathwater, saliva, mud, and the waters of a murky pool; if he can take a crust of bread and a cup of wine; if indeed he can even take empty hands and crown them with all the meaning his life can bring—why can we not see how different our lives would be if we would truly yield them to him?

Looking out the window of my study, I can see in my own backyard a parable that speaks to me about life. Sitting dejectedly in the corner by the garden compost pile is my scarecrow. He is tattered and faded—evidence of his summers of defending our garden from the birds. He used to spend winter in the shed, but last fall he somehow just didn't get put away. He stayed on the fence until about February, when a windstorm blew him off and into the cornstalks. When spring came, I dragged him to a corner of the yard, and there he would have stayed—if not for Jason. Jason Runyon and his sister, Loren, had come to spend a couple of nights with us while their parents took the church youth group on a trip to Canada. Jason had a great time fighting with this ex-protector of the harvest. He punched him and pummeled him and jumped on him and finally left him to die out beyond the back sidewalk. After Jason and Loren had gone home, I rescued the vanquished warrior from the field of battle and carried him back to the house.

He really deserved a little better treatment. Leigh and I made him one spring. He was a genuine, life-sized, fully dressed (from straw hat to shoes) scarecrow. I did the body work. With a "skin" of fence wire stretched over a "skeleton" of tomato stake sticks, and some padding here and there made out of some plastic dry-cleaning bags he was ready for clothes. Leigh made the head out of a pillowcase and painted on a handsome face. He was a scarecrow of above average intelligence, too, because we used the *Wall Street Journal* for brains. He was a worthy addition to our garden and had done his job well. He was so lifelike that people who passed by would often wave to him thinking it was me sitting on the garden fence. Once when Mike was home for a visit, he opened the door to the shed and almost jumped out of his skin when he saw the scarecrow. Even lying out in the yard, where one of Jason's solid left hooks had knocked him, he looked so real that Peg thought I had collapsed on the way to the house. The way his arm used to swing in the breeze that first summer made him look almost alive.

But, of course, he was not. He never was alive and never will be. He couldn't ever get off the fence on his own and take a walk or do a dance in the morning sunlight. He couldn't ever sing a song, or write a poem, or pull a weed, or plant a row, or take a bite out of one of those Tennessee tomatoes.

My scarecrow has the form but there isn't any substance. No life is there. He is a ragged reminder that we, too, need to have the touch of Christ to become alive. Without him we are like scarecrows watching over little patches of ground which have been entrusted to us—sitting on our fences, never knowing what makes beans sprout and corn grow and birds fly and rabbits eat lettuce. Without him we would think that the sun rises and sets somewhere around our own little fence corners—never really laughing, never really caring, never really alive.

Jesus can touch us. He can bring life to us. He calls us to live in his life-giving fellowship.

6

Unless You Want
to Know God

"Take hold of the eternal life to which you were called . . ."

What happens to people who pray is that their inward life gradually takes over from their outward life. This is not to say that they are any less active. They may be competent lawyers, doctors, businessmen. But their hearts lie in the inner life and they are moved by that.

Emilie Griffin[1]

6
Unless You Want to Know God

My heart was bubbling over. It was spring in Tennessee. If you have ever been in Tennessee in the spring, you wouldn't be happy living anywhere else. The Bradford pear trees in the front yard appeared to be in a race with the buttercups to see which could burst into bloom first. And I had been out in the yard scratching in the dirt, getting ready for all the plants and things I hoped to buy the next weekend at the home and garden show at the fairgrounds.

But mostly my heart was full from Homecoming. Just that morning I had asked Peggy how she liked her new husband. "New?" she asked, looking at my same old body slouched in my same old corduroys. "Yes, new, I was born again at Barkley."

As I have said before, I am a retreater at heart. Retreats and campmeetings have formed a very significant part of my religious heritage. Many of my weekends away from home each year are spent retreating somewhere with some group of people or another. I think I know a little about what it takes to make a retreat worthwhile and hopefully even life-changing. I have seen enough stuff done, and unfortunately, enough important things left undone, to have some definite ideas about what makes for a good retreat.

With all these things in mind—the do's and the don'ts—we had planned a retreat. My sons, Robert and Mike, Peg's sister Bo, and some friends, Matt Steinhauer and Cindy Morton, rounded out the planning crew with Peg and me. All of us had all worked together on retreats when we were in the publishing business, getting choir directors, artists, writers, or bookstore dealers together for a few days or so of retreat.

We were excited about our retreat. We made what we felt were good plans for our "Homecoming." At the end of that weekend, we were all aware that some very real things had happened among us. There was a warm openness among those of us who met together, and a deep vitality that a committee can plan and hope for, but which only the Spirit can bring. Looking back I think we should have been more attentive to the ways of the Spirit all along.

In reliving those hours of retreat the thing that stands out the most in my mind is the altar. Now I am no stranger to an altar. I grew up in a church that made use of its altar. Along with the pulpit, it was the single most important piece of furniture in the sanctuary. Of course, back in the fifties we weren't nearly so sophisticated and we just called our "sanctuary" the auditorium. But even then, and maybe especially so, the altar occupied a central place in the building and in our services.

In our church we also used the baptismal pool regularly, even though it entailed taking the benches out of the choir loft and removing some sections of the floor to get to the dark, moist regions below. I can still smell the faint, watery scent of creosote that wafted up from the ancient timbers that supported it.

There was some mystery and excitement about the baptismal service, but it was the "altar call" that struck the most fear in a teenager's heart. It remains the scene most indelibly etched in my memory. I can still hear the pleading invitations of Brother Wise over the plaintive strains of "Tell Mother I'll Be There" or the equally unnerving "Almost Persuaded" sung by my dad and the trio. And while all this was going on, Sister Mary Smith would be working the room to press the invitation home to reluctant sinners. She always felt there was work to be done in the alcove where I would sit with my buddies. With her shaking hand on our arms, and the words, "almost but lost," ringing in our ears, we had to take a death grip on the pew in front of us to remain committed to a life of sin.

Even now the altar holds a central place in the life and worship of our congregations. A few months ago a pastor over in Arkansas was showing me through the new sanctuary his growing congregation had just completed. I walked up on the platform to get the view from the pulpit and I looked out over the padded pews, deep pile carpeting, and stained glass windows. There was a beautiful altar making its graceful way across the front of the church. The corner of my eye caught one little touch that would probably have seemed incongruous to an outsider. But a regular attender would have understood. For built into the back of the altar every so often there was a place for a box of tissue. We still go forward and we still need to blow our noses and we still need to wipe the tears from our eyes when we kneel at the altar to fashion the deep decisions of our lives.

So I know about altars. I've even preached about them. Abraham's dramatic story has always especially moved me because he stopped to build an altar almost everywhere he went. He built one east of Bethel and another at Hebron near the great trees of Mamre. Perhaps the most significant one was at Moriah, where he and his young son Isaac gathered wood and brush for the final test of faith in the God who had made promises to Abraham so many years before. But I had never built an altar myself until that Homecoming weekend.

I picked up Mike and Tom at the airport to get ready to go to Barkley. Tom left us to go see his mother and his girlfriend, although I am not sure that is the order in which he made his visits. Mike and I rented a van and drove out to Dad's place and picked up some lumber that he had discarded. There were a number of redwood boards and posts and some big, heavy, old poplar beams. The beams had come out of the old Donelson house out Gallatin Road by Two Mile Pike. One of the Donelson girls, Rachel, you history buffs will remember, married Andrew Jackson. I loved the rugged character of those old timbers. The house itself had been torn down to make room for a discount store.

We took all this along with us to build our altar. There was a prominent place in the retreat schedule for private prayer and devotion. We wanted to begin each day early and end it late in quiet and solitude. We wanted a private, worshipful place where it would be good to do this. There was a building about a hundred yards or so away from everything else that had a large room which we could use as a prayer chapel. Since shared accomplishments have a way of binding people together (an old retreater's idea), we wanted everyone to join in setting up the chapel the first afternoon.

At the close of the first session, everyone had begun to get acquainted and size each other up. We told them we were going to build an altar and divided into three groups: altar builders, cross builders, and the rest of us, unskilled laborers who went out into the Kentucky woods and gathered stones to build an altar table.

At first, it was not at all unlike something I might have helped to plan. It was rather disorganized and there was a lot of noise and milling around. Probably more than one person, myself included, wondered what was going to happen here. But gradually the altar bench itself began to take form. Starting almost in the center of the room, it fanned out in all directions so there would be room for all of us to kneel together if we wanted to. Then the second group came struggling in carrying a huge cross fashioned out of the old beams. When they raised it in the center of the altar, we took the stones and mounded them around the bottom until at last it stood towering over us all. As a finishing touch we scattered straw all the way around the altar so that it would be a warm and comfortable place to be. It gradually became apparent we were building something that was going to have rich meaning to us in the next few days.

When we finished our task we crowded around our altar and knelt in the straw. With the cross standing tall above us in the piled-up stones from a Kentucky hillside, we dedicated the place and ourselves to our Father for the weekend. We had built an altar.

To be perfectly honest with you, we did not know exactly what we were going to do with out newly built sanctuary—or more accurately, what it was going to do with us. In fact, that morning before anyone had registered, the staff had gone over to the empty building and we had each voiced our ideas about how the altar should be used when it was finished. There were a couple of people present with a more liturgical background and one person who had been to several retreats at Catholic monasteries. They concluded that we should pull the shades, light a candle or two on the altar and let it be a place of silence and prayer. There were some others who had been brought up in a more experiential kind of worship. They felt that we would all soon get tired of sitting or kneeling there in silence and we would have to have some singing and some exhortation—or at least some music. About all we knew was that we wanted it to be a holy place. We even thought about putting up a sign that said "No Talking." We would place it where everyone could see it as they started up the sidewalk through the woods to the chapel. We never really reached any agreement. As it turned out we didn't need to, for the place had a character of its own, one that was to mold and shape us all as we came and went throughout the weekend.

The mood and the very presence of that chapel is aptly described by Elizabeth C. Clephane in her hymn, *Beneath the Cross of Jesus:*

> Upon the cross of Jesus
>   My eyes at times can see
> The very dying form of one
>   Who suffered there for me;
> And, from my smitten heart with tears,
>   Two wonders I confess—
> The wonders of His glorious love
>   And my unworthiness.

I grew up in a verbal, singing, sometimes even shouting, demonstrative kind of spirituality. I was not used to deep, worshipful silence. But I had come to that Homecoming weekend from the busy, noisy world with which we are all so familiar. So the silent, healing peace of that place came upon me like a gentle rain. It did not seem proper to end the day without going there. Even six o'clock in the morning did not seem too early to begin the day there in its sanctity. I think I came away determined to be an altar-builder.

So I brought home some of the lumber and the beams, and, hopefully, some of the spirit, and I was ready to get right to the task. I found that it is a lot easier to build an altar at a retreat center than it is at home. It just seems more appropriate when everybody else is there to help and nobody has to go to school or to work or run a carpool or take music lessons or answer the telephone and the doorbell. But altar-building in the real world of commerce and traffic and earning a living is a different matter. There really doesn't seem to be an appropriate place at home or at the office or in the backyard for a large wooden altar.

Altars in Everyday Places

I received some help about the true location for a personal altar from a borrowed book. When Dr. Reuben Job was still in Nashville at Upper Room he was kind enough to loan me some books from his library. This was before his election as Bishop in the United Methodist Church. I almost kept them because I know so few bishops and I thought it would be nice to have some books borrowed from one. But this seemed to be such a fleeting claim to fame that I bundled them up and returned them to him at his new address.

One of them was entitled *Poustinia—Christian Spirituality of the East for Western Man*. The word *poustinia* is a Russian word meaning desert. The writer, Catherine de hueck Doherty, said that if she were still a schoolgirl in Russia and her geography teacher asked her to name a desert she might have said, "Saharskaya Poustinia"—the Sahara Desert. But to a Russian the word means much more than a geographical place. It also means a quiet, lonely place people wish to enter to find the God who dwells within them. And while *poustinia* meant truly isolated, lonely places to which specially called people would go as hermits, it was also used as a name for special places people had reserved in their homes to which they might go to pray and meditate. A person who lived in a secluded spot was called a "poustinik."

The book itself is about her present work in Canada in a community known as Madonna House. Those who live there lead a life based on prayer, work, silence, and honest love for all those who visit there for prayer and retreat. Though the book tells the story of the founding of a place where people may go for periods of their lives she describes the real nature of *poustinia* in an early chapter. She writes, "It is vitally important at the outset to emphasize that there is no need for a log cabin, cottages, huts, in order to lead a life of prayer. Prayer is interior. The hut, the cabin, the chapel, is the human heart in which we must learn how to pray. Solitude sometimes helps prayer, and for special vocations is the cradle of prayer, and powerful prayer at that. But for the average Christian, prayer doesn't need a geographical spot. Prayer is a contact of love between God and man."[2]

She goes on to write, "Deserts, silence, solitudes are not necessarily places but states of heart and mind. These deserts can be found in the midst of the city, and in the every day of our lives. We need only to look for them and realize our tremendous need for them. They will be small solitudes, little deserts, tiny pools of silence, but the experience they will bring, if we are disposed to enter them, may be as exultant and as holy as all the deserts of the world, even the one God himself entered. For it is God who makes solitude, deserts and silences holy."[3]

While it may be true that the daily arena of our lives is the place where it is the most difficult to "build an altar," it is still the place where it is supposed to be erected. Most of us can maintain some kind of spiritual inclination for a weekend or so while on a retreat. Maybe we can appear pious and even holy. But life in Christ is not a life that is supposed to be lived apart from our everydays. Indeed, as Henri J.M. Nouwen writes, ". . . the spiritual life can only be real when it is lived in the midst of the pains and the joys of the here and now."[4]

I am sure it is true that anyone can turn to God in solitude and prayer at almost any point or place in his everyday life. But the fact remains that most of us do not know how to do so. We all know that Jesus has come to live within us and we know that he never leaves us. What we have not learned very well is how to live our lives with our focus on him. It took the building of an altar up in Kentucky to show me and the rest of us how to turn ourselves inward to where he dwells. It was a graphic demonstration of how to "take hold of the life" that he brings—a demonstration of how badly we needed to learn to be altarbuilders in our hearts.

Demands and Disciplines

The process of inner "altar building" or spiritual formation, as some students of the deeper life term it, has been likened to a journey in two directions. Evelyn Underhill says oldtimers described the two as *mortification* and *prayer*. Perhaps a pair of more up-to-date words to guide us on our quest are *discipline* and *desire*. Whatever the processes are called, they first encompass one's turning into the reality of God. Then there follows a constant seeking to bring one's own self into total compliance with this deeper reality.

I am convinced that one of the reasons most of us are not very good at altar building is that we evangelical Protestant-types have too much confidence in our own will power. We seem to be so sure that we will be able to maintain our life in God that we do not believe we need any aids or symbols to call us to pray. I don't think we have enough sacraments or rituals. We do not have many reminders to keep us setting ourselves to the task of the spiritual life.

In the Old Testament God seemed very careful to provide the Israelites with signs and customs that would continually keep them from forgetting their first obligation to love him.

Two of the most unique Jewish symbols which have testified since ancient times to the eternal Covenant between God and Israel are the *tefillin* and the *mezuzah*. Both of them are capsule reminders of the entire law which the Jew was bidden to observe. They were suggested by the words from a passage of the Old Testament:

> Hear, O Israel: The Lord our God, the Lord is one. Love the Lord your God with all your heart and with all your soul and with all your strength. These commandments that I give you today are to be upon your hearts. Impress them upon your children. Talk about them when you sit at home and when you walk along the road, when you lie down and when you get up. Tie them as symbols on your hands and bind them on your foreheads. Write them on the doorframes of your houses and on your gates (Deut. 6:4–9).

The *tefillin*, a name coming from the same root word as the Hebrew word for prayer, *tefilah*, consisted of two small black boxes. One was bound on the hand and one on the head. They were worn only on weekdays to serve as a reminder to the Jew of the commandments at the time when he was beset and burdened by the cares of life and might be tempted to forget.

The other Jewish practice that grew out of this passage was a *mezuzah*. *Mezuzah* is the Hebrew word for doorpost, but it is also the name given to a far more significant custom.

I first read about a *mezuzah* a couple of summers back when I was in Colorado. The Denver evening paper noted that a local Boy's Club was getting ready to expand their facilities. To do so they had purchased an old house adjoining their property, and they were getting ready to tear it down to make room for their addition. Someone protested, claiming the old house had historical significance. In fact, they said, it was of international importance. Golda Meir, the lady who rose to fame as Prime Minister of Israel, had lived in the house with her sister and brother-in-law when she was going to high school. It had not worked out too happily and she had returned to Michigan to finish school, but she had lived in the old house for a time. I'm not sure how it came out—whether the historians or the progressives prevailed.

One of the things discovered in the house that indicated a Jewish family had lived there was the place for the *mezuzah* carved into the doorposts. From time immemorial, it has marked the Jewish home and made it identifiable as a residence where Jews lived. There was a small opening near the upper third of the right hand side of the door as you entered. A small cylinder was placed in the opening, and inside it there was a scroll. On one side of the scroll there were the words from Deuteronomy as quoted above. On the back side, there was only one word, *Shaddai*, a Hebrew word for God. Near the top of the cylinder there was a small hole and the scroll was placed so that the word *Shaddai* could be seen.

Upon entering or leaving the house, a pious Jew would take the tip of his fingers and touch the *mezuzah* exactly on the word *Shaddai*. Then he would press them to his lips and pray, "May God keep watch over my going out and my coming in, now and forevermore."

The Jews have a legend about Artaban, the pagan king of

Parthia. He sent a famous rabbi, Rabbi Judah ha Nasi, a gift of a splendid pearl. The sage responded with a gift of his own—a *mezuzah*. The king was outraged by what he considered to be a mockery of him and he angrily rebuked the rabbi. "See how you have insulted me. I sent you a gift of great value and you reciprocate with a trifle of no value at all."

The rabbi explained, "What you do not understand is this. The gift you gave me is of such great value that I will have to stay awake at night to guard it. On the other hand, the gift that I gave you will guard you, even when you are asleep!"

I do not have a *mezuzah* on my doorpost. I probably go out the door in the morning just like you do—late. Or I go out to start the car when the weather is cold. I go out to chase the neighbor's dog out of the petunias in the spring, to get the newspaper, or to pick up a tin can in the yard thrown from a passing car. Hardly ever do I go out the door with a prayer. But it would be a wonderful thing to have something to remind me as I leave the house that I am only able to go because of the health and strength which God gives—a symbol to make me recall when I return that it is only because of his watchcare and protection. I need something on the doorpost to keep me ever mindful that only he can mercifully watch between me and those I am leaving behind while I am away. Most of all, I need a reminder so that I would always recall that if I do not return, he alone can someday unite us all in his heavenly home.

The lesson that both the *tefillin* and the *mezzuzah* were supposed to teach, of course, was that one was to live all of the days of their lives in the love and watchcare of the Father. They were enjoined to love the Lord with all their hearts and souls and strength. But it was also a commandment to be obeyed all the time. It was to be kept when they got up in the morning and when they went to bed at night. It was to be observed when they were at home and when they were away. Always they were to be careful "that you do not forget the Lord . . ." (Deut. 6:12).

Probably an aid to disciplining oneself to pray which we are all more familiar with is the sign of the cross. I always dread to see a player on the team I'm not rooting for using the sign of the cross before stepping to the foul line to shoot the potential tying and game-winning points. I don't believe it always works, but I wish he wouldn't do it anyway—just in case it might work this time.

The other day I read that the prayer behind the sign of the cross was something like this:

> God be in my head,
> God be in my heart,
> God be to the left of me,
> God be to the right of me.

I am not suggesting that every time the sign of the cross is used this prayer is actually prayed. Catholics are probably just as susceptible to going through the motions as Protestants are. But if you are like me, and I am fairly sure you are, we both need to pray that prayer about every twenty minutes for the rest of our lives. And it wouldn't hurt to have something to remind us to do it either, would it?

He has come to live in us. Still, it is up to us to learn ways of constant recognition, acknowledgment, and fellowship that will allow us to live with our roots planted deeply into him. Maybe for awhile, we will have to make the sign of the cross in our pockets . . . or put a *mezzuzah* on the backporch doorpost where the neighbors won't see us as we pause to pray . . . or tie a string around our fingers . . . or pin notes on our mittens. But somehow, we must learn to take hold of the life to which we have been called. In any discussion of spiritual progress the word "discipline" nearly always emerges. We must build some patterns and habits that will, through their daily repetition, slowly but surely free us from living on the surface and turn us deeply inward to the peace and strength that he alone can bring.

Annie Dillard has a word or two for us here which I cannot leave out. They are from her book, *Teaching a Stone to Talk*. She writes about the function of discipline in spiritual formation: "God needs nothing, asks nothing, and demands nothing, like the stars. It is a life with God which demands these things. . . . You do not have to do these things—unless you want to know God. They work on you, not on him. . . . You do not have to sit outside in the dark. If, however, you want to look at the stars, you will find that darkness is necessary. But the stars neither require nor demand it."[5] (Thank you, Annie.)

Hungers and Thirsts

I guess the part discipline must play in our spiritual development is understood well enough, for it figures into every other area of our lives. No skill, it seems, comes to us without a price. But the other word that occurs just as often in discussions about life in the spirit is not as easily understood. We do not fathom its meanings as readily because it is too often not a word in our experience. But it is a term the saints often use. Strangely enough, once they begin to use it they speak less and less of having to discipline themselves into patterns of prayer and devotion. The word is "desire."

"Desire," as a word, probably doesn't carry as strong a set of meanings to us as does the word "discipline." Discipline is a kind of a tough, unbending word. It resists attempts to round off its edges. And it doesn't want to hang around with qualifiers like nearly or partly or half. It either wants to be used like it is or be left alone. Desire, though, comes in such a variety of shapes and strengths that one has to study it some each time to understand its meaning.

Jesus used the words "hunger" and "thirst" when he was describing the quality of our desire for the reality of the life in God. But in our day these words depict appetites gratified so amply and so frequently that we hardly know what they mean anymore.

A couple of winters ago, I was in a motel in South Carolina trying to write a short essay on the beatitude about hungering and thirsting after righteousness. When I had arrived at the motel there was a basket of fruit, crackers and candy in the room. Down the balcony were drink, snack, and ice machines. There was a *Shoney's* next door, a *McDonald's* nearby, and a *Bojangles* across the street.

My schedule on the road that week was about the same as usual. I would try to get up around seven to study and work an hour or so before eating breakfast. That week there was a small prayer and study group at the church at eleven and then some friendly members were taking turns feeding the pastor, his wife, and the "evangelist." There must have been some kind of a "cookoff" because it seemed that each day the meals got bigger and better. In the afternoons, I studied and read before supper and the service. Someone took me out for a snack afterward and I just ate something light with them—like a hot fudge sundae.

Needless to say, I was having a bit of difficulty in coming to a way of understanding and expressing the deep meanings Jesus must have had when he spoke of our quest for righteousness in terms of hunger and thirst. I think he was trying to ask us how much we really want goodness. Somehow, the thing we need to hear in the word desire is something about its intensity. Is it like a starving man who wants something to eat? Or like a man dying of thirst who wants a drink of water? Is it a desire that is compelling and life-ordering?

Desire would bring about a quiet, almost unnoticed change in the very sources out of which our prayer springs. It would be the beginning of a difference in our prayers. No longer would we pray because we feel the necessity to pray—but we would be praying because the thought of spending the day without the companionship of the Father has become unthinkable.

We sometimes speak of *waiting on the Lord.* By this we probably mean that we have brought our needs to him, possibly suggested the best way for him to answer, and now we are waiting on his action in our behalf. There is another term in the Old Testament that is in marked contrast. Sometimes people were said to be *waiting upon the Lord.* The matter of prayer for them had passed beyond merely what *he could do for them.* Instead, their prayer now was centered in their desire to be what *they could be to him.*

The light on the faces of those who pray out of desire, the very radiance of their words, written or spoken, is unmistakably bright. It is not so much what they claim to have attained. Often, they lament the weakness of their desire. Rather, it is in the adoration and praise with which they speak of what they have seen and felt.

Sometimes when I am working upstairs in my study I will hear Peg down in the kitchen with the measuring cups and the mixing bowls. Then there will be the sounds of the mixer in the house. And I hear the oven door opening and a pan sliding on the shelf. After a while, there comes wafting up the backsteps the sweet aroma of a lemon pound cake with apricot nectar baking in the oven. (For my money it is hard to do anything wrong with a lemon or an apricot.) There is the faint sound of the confectioner's sugar icing bubbling in a pan on top of the stove. I hear the oven door open and shut for the last time and I hear her tapping the pan until the cake comes out on the antique cake stand. Then I know she will be pouring that hot sugary icing over the cake. I can almost see it running down the sides and piling up in little puddles on the stand. I am listening very attentively now as she washes the pans and bowls and puts them on the drainer to dry. And she leaves the kitchen. Suddenly, I need a drink of water. In the kitchen, I look carefully in all directions. Then I reach around on the back side and pinch off some of that warm, moist cake. And the icing gets all over my fingers. Usually I find that I have pinched off some cake about the same place where Peg had already taken a pinch before she left the kitchen.

Obviously, I don't have any rules for this ritual nor do I need any. I don't make myself listen to her progress. And I don't have to force myself to show up when she is gone from the kitchen. There isn't any discipline involved at all. (Lack of discipline, maybe.) The explanation is clear enough. I just love cake—especially warm, lemon pound cake made with apricot nectar with sugary icing still oozing down the sides.

I have known a few people and I have read of others who talk about God with the same excitement and delight that I use to describe warm cake. These truly devout people speak of coming to a place where turning to him is the finest thing that happens in the day. Not because they should—although they should. Not because it is necessary—although it is necessary. Not because they feel they have to—although one really has to. But because they want to. They truly *desire* him. They pause at the doorpost to pray because they have come to the place in their lives where they have learned that going somewhere without him is like not going anywhere at all.

The lives of people who have truly loved God are filled with stories of their struggles and strivings to build altars and maintain spiritual discipline. But they also will tell you of mornings when they were waiting on the porch for the sun to come up because they could not wait to meet him.

Our success in turning inward into his life will depend upon both our persistence in disciplining ourselves and on the quality of our desire to know God and to love him.

Deep inside our life there must be a holy, dedicated place where an altar stands and he alone is worshiped, a quiet, solitary place where only his voice can be heard.

We must become altar builders.

7

No Minor Matters

"You . . . were called to be free."

GALATIANS 5:13

Have you ever noticed that to be rich always means to be impoverished on another level? It is enough for you to say, "I have this watch, it is mine," and close your hand on it, to be in possession of a watch and to have lost a hand. And if you close your mind on riches, if you close your heart so that you can keep it safe, never lose it, then it becomes as small as the thing on which you have closed yourself in.

ANTHONY BLOOM[1]

7

No Minor Matters

I was brought up in a denomination that spent a great part of its energy and efforts in defining and avoiding worldliness. It has always seemed to me that it was easier for some of those old-time preachers and evangelists to identify worldliness back in my early days. Most often it was thought of as something the women wore—or didn't wear. Fortunately, as I recall it, women's clothing was not an issue that our pastor dealt with very often. He generally stated his philosophy on this matter by indicating he thought if a barn needed painting it should be painted.

In our local church though, there were other matters about which the body deliberated and made pronouncements. I can remember some of these issues which seemed to be "burning" at the time. Once, one of the truly godly men of the church, who taught a class of high school boys, felt that it would be good to organize a softball team and play in the church league at Shelby Park. Someone else in the church persuaded the company where he was employed to donate some used uniforms for the team to wear. The only request made by the company, a manufacturer of candy, was that the church leave the name of various candy bars on the backs of the shirts. For this reason I played right field for a couple of years with GOO GOO on my back.

The matter was taken to the church board to see if it would be all right to put the name of the church on the front of the shirts. Much discussion ensued. It was finally decided that it would be better if the team used the class name on the uniform instead of the name of the church. So the team played as "Victory Class" those early years (although I don't remember that we had very many victories in the beginning). We kept getting beat by churches that had resolved the question of softball-playing many years before, churches that had decided they would use the church name—and by one church in particular which had also decided it would be all right if their first baseman chewed tobacco.

Finally we did begin to play with the church name on our uniforms and even won our share of championships, although the right fielder had been replaced by the time all this occurred. And chewing tobacco never was approved for the first baseman or anyone else on the team.

I remember another semi-crisis that came along in the life of the church in the mid-forties. My dad was the songleader at the time and he was very good at getting the people to sing. He was a spontaneous director who loved to change songs and tempos frequently without giving much of a warning to anyone. But with Elizabeth Pate at the piano and two or three good strong sopranos and altos on the front row of the choir watching his every move, the rest of the congregation followed whether they meant to or not.

When he had assumed his duties with the volunteer choir, he had also inherited a volunteer orchestra. He always had trouble keeping the orchestra with him as he would weave songs into medleys and moods during the song service. With his customary ingenuity, he came upon a solution to this challenge to his leadership. The church should buy an organ. But when this was taken to the board, some of the members were less than excited. And it was not just because of the price. Many of them had left so-called "formal" churches to come to this place where the services were warm and expressive. All those churches from which they had come had organs. In time, of course, our church joined the march of progress and today it would not seem like church without an organ.

A first reaction might be that the church had ill-spent its time in debating such minor matters as softball shirts and Hammond organs. Perhaps I thought so, too, at the time. But there was something deeper going on here—something that I was going to come to appreciate more and more. For in the quest to be a holy people there are no minor matters. To be taught early that nothing is neutral in the life of the spirit was to be apprised of a deep and inviolate spiritual principle.

Called to Difference

It has been suggested by John Stott in his book, *Christian Counter Culture*, that the key verse of the Sermon on the Mount is "Do not be like them" (Matt. 6:8). This does indeed seem to be the underlying theme. There is hardly a paragraph in the Sermon in which the life of the Christian is not shown to be in contrast. Sometimes it is with the Gentiles or the heathen, and sometimes with the Jews or the religious people. The Christian life is described as an on-going choice of one way as over against another. There are two roads, two gates, two masters, two treasures, two ways of seeing, two preoccupations in life, and finally, two ways to respond to his words.

The Sermon is a system of Christian values, ethical standards, and religious practices that are to find expression in all of one's life and lifestyle. They are totally at variance with the life of those who are not attempting to base their lives on the teachings of Christ. And the thought expressed in the Sermon is the essential theme of the Bible.

In the Old Testament, God set out to call a people to himself. And the words of Jesus, "Do not be like them," are giving the same call to difference as the words God used when he told the people of Israel, "I am the Lord your God. You must not do as they do in Egypt, where you used to live, and you must not do as they do in the land of Canaan, where I am bringing you. Do not follow their practices" (Lev. 18:1–3).

In the verses that follow the words in Galatians that I have quoted at the beginning of this chapter, Paul is also emphasizing that there are two separate and distinct ways of conduct which a person may exhibit. He contrasts them as ways of living either by the Spirit or in the flesh. Paul, though a great theologian, was an intensely practical man and he usually ended his letters with a very down-to-earth appeal that the truth might be lived out. This is the way he concludes the letter to the churches in Galatia.

One of Paul's foundational theological truths was his declaration that Christ had brought the reign of law to an end and replaced it with a reign of grace. The danger in preaching this kind of freedom was the possibility that some would reason this meant they were now free to do anything they wanted to do. Paul tells them that they are indeed "called to be free" but he now enjoins them to use that freedom to live their lives in the Spirit.

The question which always must be grappled with is what the call to "difference" means. What was Jesus saying when he said that we were not to be like them? And what was God trying to get the Israelites not to do so they would not be like those in Egypt or in Canaan? It is always the question that those who would follow Christ must be asking among themselves. And the answer must be somehow shaped and formulated to resist the peculiar temptations and pressures of a changing society.

I think most of us would acknowledge that we are thoroughly conditioned by the society in which we live. Our hopes, songs, actions, words and thoughts are constantly bombarded by our culture. One morning last spring I was going across a campground to speak in a retreat service. I think I like morning services best of all and, as well as I knew, my mind was ready and my heart was full. In fact, my heart was so full I was humming a song to myself as I walked along in the bright morning sunshine. You can imagine my chagrin when it dawned on me what this prayed-up, ready-to-preach-on-Christian-devotion speaker was humming—"Welcome to Millertime." Well, it is a catchy tune and I guess that's why they wrote it as they did. For the moment I was caught.

Maybe the reason it seemed easier for the old-timers to define worldliness was that it was simply a question of not being like "them," or in abstaining from "their" practices. But with the advent of radio and television and other means of mass media, no longer is it so easily done. It reaches beyond such matters as the name on a shirt or the manner of accompaniment for the singing of the congregation. Even deeper, it seems to me that worldliness is the spirit of our day. It is our being totally at home here. It is our inability to care. It is a lack of shame or indignation. Things would be so much simpler if it were only a matter of wearing black socks. But Jesus reminded us that the exterior of our lives is only the expression of the spirit within us.

Job makes an interesting commentary on his day when he writes that the "men pasture stolen flocks, they drive away the orphan's donkey and they take the widow's ox in pledge" (Job 24:2–3). Since each of these acts was a specific deed they could be categorized and avoided. And they could be made right. But another thing was happening that must have caused even greater confusion and difficulty. Job notes that "men move boundary stones" (Job 24:2). And with the markers, or the dividers, no longer in the right place it became impossible to decide where the boundaries should be drawn. There was no reference point.

Maybe that describes our present day. The lines that once divided us from the ones whom we were not supposed to be like do not seem to be very plain any more.

We are all confronted by the differences between us and the life of God. Often they are not so much inclinations to perform some evil deed as they are our conformance to the spirit of the day. It is this spirit that forms the foundation of our inability to live the life of God, or rather, our failure to let the life of God possess us.

I want to address two telling characteristics of the spirit of our day which lead us away from God. Outwardly, they can be seen in our lives as hurry and clutter. Inwardly, they reside as the spirits of impatience and of materialism. They are opposites to a spirit which is epitomized by trust and simplicity.

Hurry, Impatience, and Trust

I was reminded of the first of the two, impatience, by a conversation at our dinner table the other night. Sometimes the mealtimes themselves are saying things if we would just listen.

Tom was telling us that one of his friends had taken his girl-friend out to dinner at the best restaurant in town. Tom was expressing amazement because it had cost the two of them $135.00 to eat that evening. But something else was causing Tom even more consternation. It was the fact that it took them 3 hours and 45 minutes to eat this $135 meal. Tom said, "Any-thing that costs that much ought to be ready when you get there."

It may be that one of the deepest signs of worldliness in us all is that we are watching the same clock society uses. Martin E. Marty describes most of us when he writes in his book, *A Cry of Absence:* "In the culture of welfare . . . a populace has acquired a taste for 'entitlements' contrary to the trends of most of the rest of history of the human race, inhabitants of such culture de-mand and see their right to basic satisfactions: minimum wages, housing, social security, and the like. . . . But many people carry over the sense of entitlement into the spiritual realm. Nothing should be denied them. Universe, world, God, they seem to say, you owe me that quick fix, the sunshine in the heart, the readi-ness to smile."[2]

It seems we have lost all of the concept of the working rela-tionship that exists between quality and time. We Americans are activists and doers. It is our nature to roll up our sleeves and get the job done. And heaven help anything or anyone that gets in the way. Problems are to be solved and schedules are to be met. Time is of the essence to us.

All this is not so alien to those of us who are in the body of Christ, either. Last year Peg and I were up in Virginia for her Aunt Pauline's funeral. We are not any more ready for death than we are for living—and it always seems to catch most of us with lots to do. We arrived at the motel late that night, bleary-eyed and exhausted, after a day and a half of rushing around getting ready to go. Almost too tired to sleep, we turned on the TV and were greeted on the religious network by an old ac-quaintance from my gospel music business days. He had slipped into a new role as TV host—and also into a new hairdo. So we stayed with him until he waved good-by an hour or so later.

One of his guests reminded me about this impatience thing. He was a very handsome and impressive young minister of the gospel. And he had a powerful story to tell. Even as a boy he had held preaching services in his own backyard. From that modest beginning a large congregation had been born. But the reason for his being on the program on this particular evening was to tell of an occasion of healing in his own life.

Some time before, he had been holding a revival in his own church. During this meeting he had begun to have problems with his throat and with his speaking voice. From listening to him on the program it was apparent that he preached with power and enthusiasm. We could imagine his use of his deep, pleasant voice as he expounded the gospel, exhorted the believers, and confronted the unrighteous. When he went to see a physician he was told that he should not even carry on a conversation for three months. Ninety days of silence was not something that he thought would be worthwhile for him to be doing. So he went immediately to his study where he began to pray, "Heal me, God, I do not have three months." And he was healed and went on with the meeting.

I think maybe I had better let you know just here that I am not writing about his healing. I believe it occurred as he told it. And I can rejoice with him for his trust in God and for the miracle of healing itself. Since I am quite sure I would not be around to be writing a book if it were not for the healing power of God, I want to say that I believe in healing. But I do want to comment about his clock, and about what I think it is saying about his, and our, patience and trust.

Can you imagine telling God—the God in whom there is no beginning and no ending, the eternal, always was and always will be God, the God who buries tulip bulbs in the darkness of the soil, the God who hides oak trees in acorns, this God—that you don't have three months? It seems bold to me, to say the very least, to say this to God, who knew you long before you ever came to be. To suggest to this God—who has promised to gather up all of your life and transform it into the goodness of his purpose—to get on with it because you don't have time to dilly-dally around, is pretty daring!

I can almost hear God saying, "I think I'll just heal him. It will be easier than explaining it to him." But I would like to have suggested to this preacher that God could probably teach him more in three months of "hush" than he could learn in thirty years of listening to himself.

Thomas Merton once told a friend to quit trying so hard in prayer. He reminded him, "How does an apple ripen? It just sits in the sun." Which prompted the hearer to write, "A small green apple cannot ripen in one night by tightening all its muscles, squinting its eyes and tightening its jaws in order to find itself the next morning miraculously red, ripe, and juicy beside all its counterparts. Like the birth of a baby, or the opening of a rose, the birth of true self takes place in God's time. We must wait for God. . . ."[3]

But waiting is not easy for us nine-to-fivers. Last fall I was up in the mountains of New Mexico for a week. Early in the week I addressed a group of pastors. When they departed to go back to their respective labors, I stayed on to meet with a group of their parishioners who came in a day and a half later. My life that week took on a very relaxed, orderly, quiet posture. There was time to read and to write, to walk and to pray. I went on walks in the woods and to concerts played by mountain streams splashing across grassy meadows. I saw art shows put on by wild flowers in glorious whites and pinks and purples. There were no telephones, televisions, or radios. Silence and solitude became welcome companions.

Having secured a little bit of serenity with even so tenuous a grasp, I found myself wondering why the rest of these retreaters drove their cars back and forth between the lodge and the dining hall—and why they rushed off to play golf or tennis or go shopping back in town. It seemed to me, as the self-proclaimed guru of the week, that they attacked every hour of the retreat as if their coming could only be justified by thoroughly filling every moment. They gave trophies for golf and horseshoes and volleyball and for the skits and the games. But there were no prizes or premiums for naps or walks in the woods or for stillness. From my new-found place of quietness, I pondered all their ant-like scurrying.

Then I remembered how I had come to this place in the mountains. I had spent three exhausting and frantic days prior to arriving here. I had spoken three times the first day, driven almost all of the second, and flown across the country on the third to be here to talk to these people about slowing down the pace of their lives. On the last Sunday, I was planning to close the sermon and a car door at about the same time and hurry to the airport in Albuquerque some three hours away to catch the first plane I could to get home.

I am beginning to get a sneaking suspicion that some things will only come to us by waiting—that some things will never happen for us because we are in too big a hurry to let the time go by in which they can come true. We are not very patient people.

I often talk with people who firmly believe that God has some rich and deep purpose for their lives. It is evident they are sincere in their willingness and desire to find and fulfill that plan. But they experience difficulty because they cannot seem to trust the God who has ordained such purposes to also bring it about in his good and providential timing. They can't believe that when that something finally does occur, it will be with such obvious rightness that they will almost blush to ever have doubted it would be. They will wonder why it was so difficult to continue the present path with dedication and joy until some new word came to them.

To be able to do so we must become aware that there is some other way of accounting for time. We must begin to hear, however faintly at first, the rhythm and movement of the One who set it all in motion when the world began.

Clutter, Stuff, and Simplicity

That brings me to the other problem that I feel keeps us from our hidden completeness—the spirit which fills our lives with clutter.

Clutter seems a very descriptive word to me just now. Tom has recently gone into the lawnmowing business and the garage had to be rearranged so that there was a place for his equipment to be stored at night. This happened just as Leigh was moving back home from her apartment at college—and she needed part of the garage to store her furniture until she left again for graduate school. All of this was crammed into a garage that was already filled with a workbench, a freezer, the remnants of Peg's antique business, the garden tractor and equipment, and boxes and boxes and boxes of books. As Tom and I restacked and rearranged, we concluded that we certainly had plenty of stuff and that clutter was a good word to describe us.

Some time ago, I came across an apt description of the process of clutter and accumulation. Written by Jim Russell, an advertising man, it appeared in the American Airlines flight magazine, *The American Way*. I was interested in his account of what he called the "Sideward Leaping Technology Syndrome." By his own admission it had helped his family join the *nouveau pauvre* in easy effortless steps.

Because Jim was an old movie freak, his wife had given him a video cassette recorder so he could tape the "golden oldies" while he slept. Thus he could view them during prime time rather than watching them in the wee hours of the morning. His neighbor, with a knowing look, had remarked that the new machine would end up costing him another thousand to fifteen hundred dollars. Refusing to elaborate, the neighbor would only say, "You'll see."

A few days later Jim's son, noting that so much of what they wished to tape came over UHF channels declared, "Our antenna doesn't pick up UHF." Jim relates, "That weekend we went shopping for a new antenna and ended up investing in a combination VHF/UHF model with a coaxial cable and a signal splitter."

However, when it was installed and they all settled back to watch, somehow the picture didn't seem to look all that much better and even Jim had to admit the eight-year-old set had seen better days. Reasoning that the only way to get their money out of the new VCR was to buy a new set he said, "A mere $585 later we had a solid state color receiver with electronic tuning and automatic tint control." And they settled into a period of satisfied viewing. Everything worked. "It had cost a bit more than we expected to enter the world of video tape but nowhere near $1,000 or more. (A little quick arithmetic would have shown $725.) And besides it was worth it. Sensible choices, solid enjoyment."[4]

But the critical eye of Sideward Leaping Technology had not stopped roving. "You know," his wife said, "this room is such a clutter. What is an entertainment center?" "What it was, was $300, unfinished and knocked down, I was to discover," Jim lamented. Eventually a solid wall of shelving held all the TV-related equipment, all their books, and several *objects d'junk*, with a couple of shelves left over.

Summarizing, he put forth the following tenet, ". . . technology begats technology begats poverty."

Of course, his neighbor wasn't quite through with him yet either. On his next visit he asked, "How much?" "Not much," Jim parried. The neighbor studied it all for a moment and asked, "All done?" And Jim snapped, "Of course." His neighbor went out the door with a parting shot, "What's going on those empty shelves?"

My experience is that they will not be empty for long. And as soon as I finish writing for the day I am headed to the garage to build some more shelves. The problem seems that everything which used to be an option is now standard equipment—that our needs are always multiplying.

The late Rabbi Abraham Joshua Heschel, who was an authorative voice in the Jewish community and in the religious life of America, wrote, "The problem of living does not arise with the question of how to take care of the rascals or with the realization of how we blunder in dealing with other people. It begins in relation to our own selves, in the handling of our physiological and emotional functions. What is first at stake in the life of man is not the fact of sin, of the wrong and the corrupt, but the natural acts, the needs. Our possessions prove no less a problem than our passions. The primary task, therefore, is not how to deal with the evil, but how to deal with the neutral, how to deal with our needs. . . . Every human being is a cluster of needs. Yet these needs are not the same in all men nor unalterable in any one man. There is a fixed minimum of needs for all men, but no fixed maximum for any man. Unlike animals, man is the playground for the multiplication of needs and interests, some of which are indigenous to his nature, while others are induced by advertisement, fashion, envy, or come about as miscarriages of authentic needs."[5]

We are all familiar with this problem of escalating needs. I think that life was probably intended to be far simpler than we have allowed it to become. In the Sermon on the Mount, Jesus acknowledges that we have needs. But he also seems to be saying that the whole process is far less complicated than we imagine. Physically, he indicates that life consists of something to eat, something to wear, and something over our heads to shelter us from the elements. Psychologically, we are rather simple as well. We need someone to love, something to do, and something to look forward to. Most of us have ready access to food, clothing, shelter, love, purpose and hope. So how does our life get so cluttered, and why do we spend so much of our time worrying and so many of our weekends building new shelves in the garage?

Up the street from our house is a church with a billboard out front usually proclaiming a negative thought for the day. But the other morning, the sign cheerfully proffered some good advice, "Peace is being content with what you have."

Now I think that I am reasonably happy with what I have. At least I do not have some wish list on the back burner of my mind for a bunch of new stuff that I would like to get. So, I asked myself as I waited for the traffic signal to change, why do I seem to be missing what the sign is promising? Where is all the peace? Does it have to do with my fear of losing what I do have—or is it my worry about my ability to pay for it all? Or am I wondering if it will all last as long as I need it, or at least until the final payment? In a way, I wished the sign would have just said something negative I could have ignored, instead of reminding me of the struggle in which I always seem to find myself concerning my needs.

The struggle is real to us all. Every so often, Peg will say to me, "I've got to go to the grocery store today. There is nothing in the house to eat." Or maybe one of the boys will say it to Peg, "Mom, when are you going to the store? I'm starving to death." Sometimes I ask her to wait until later in the afternoon so I can go with her. I like to go to the store with her, so we make the big trip down to Green Hills to her favorite grocery store. I watch the people and push the buggy around behind her, backtracking occasionally for an item or two that she missed as we went along. Depending on my appetite at the time, I add an unlisted item here and there to the buggy. My observation is that it probably is better to go to the grocery when you have just eaten. When you are hungry everything looks good. Leaving Peg to check out and pay, I bring the car around to load up the five or six bags we invariably have.

When we get home, I like to help put the groceries away. I guess this is a hold-over from my supermarket, shelf-stocking night job during seminary days—or from playing store when I was a little boy. So I like to restack the soup cans and add little "grocery man" touches here and there.

The strange thing about all this is that when we get back to our house in which there was "nothing to eat," there isn't much room for the goods from our latest shopping spree. The cabinets are full, the pantry is crowded, the refrigerator is crammed, and the freezer is bulging—all overflowing with "nothing to eat." It would be funny if it did not seem to be saying something deeper about us that is probably more tragic than it is comical.

And what is true about the pantry I have found is true also about my closet. While I was in the publishing business, I didn't spend a whole lot of time budgeting the family expenditures. Like most people, I just hoped the next raise would bring us back into line. When I returned to writing and speaking it occurred to Peg and me that there was not going to be anybody to give me a raise next year—and maybe a budget would not be so bad after all. So we sat down and went through a couple of years' worth of cancelled checks to see what we had done before. Going through old checks is a revealing process, to say the least. (Humiliating is another word that comes to mind.) But in due time, we came to grips with our past and made resolves and predictions for the future.

Thus it was that I found myself with a clothing budget. It was not a particularly exorbitant amount, but rather what I deemed adequate in assessing my personal needs. And the truth is that I always spend my budget, plus a little more, but I don't ever buy anything that I truly need—except socks.

I remember one morning I was up early and searching without much success for a pair of matching socks to wear to an important meeting that day. So I took all the "matchless" ones out from under the bed. Then I knelt down and began to sing "Nearer My God to Thee" in a very reverent voice. Peg asked what in the world I was doing and I explained to her that I was having a memorial service for all the poor socks who had been widowed by the washer. And Peg, who can find things in the house that always seem to elude me, went to the drawer and produced a matching pair, thus bringing the memorial service to an end.

But on the whole I do not buy anything that I need because I already have shirts, shoes, pants, suits, coats, jackets, belts, swimming suits, underwear, handkerchiefs, ties, socks (even if Peggy does have to find them), and everything else I could possibly use both for modesty and comfort. But still I spend the budget. I buy some clothes because the lapels are wider, or narrower, because there was a new color this year, because I am tired of my old jacket, because I saw a new one I liked better—it's always something. But hardly ever because of need.

I hope that it is not a virtue to continue wearing a doubleknit leisure suit just because you cannot seem to wear a hole in it large enough to merit discarding it. Still, that does not seem to be quite the acceptable way to live if we let the research and development and the advertising divisions of American business define the perimeters of our need for us—especially since they make their living creating needs for the rest of us. Even now, somebody somewhere is designing a new model, something that will run faster, shred it smaller, wash it cleaner, play it more faithfully, do it in cold water, have natural shoulders, or something else that will call for trading our old one in on it.

I don't think I can tell you what your needs are. I am having enough difficulty in determining my own. But I do think it is fair to say that neither one of us will have much success in "not being like them" if we let society continually escalate our needs, real or imagined. Somehow we must find some new priority or some new stick by which to measure our lives.

Paul tells us in Galatians that the answer is to "live in the Spirit." The essence of the matter of worldliness, of "being like them," finds its meaning and its dangers in our spirits. It is true that there are wrong deeds and acts. But they are only carried out in our lives because they have taken root in our desires.

A Gracious Invitation

I particularly like Paul's choice of words here. Whether the accusation is true or not, some people have described the message of the church as being a long list of things that people could not do and places they should not go. The words that were used to picture the church were legalistic, narrow, and strict. Paul does not say that we are called to be deprived. Rather, he says that we are called to be free. And when you read the catalogue of evil deeds which are characteristic of life in the flesh (Gal. 5:19-21) and contrast them with the listing of the lovely and desirable fruits of the Spirit (Gal. 5:22), the wisdom of Paul's use of the word "freedom" is magnified.

Paul is echoing the theme of Jesus, ". . . seek first his kingdom and his righteousness and all these things will be given to you as well" (Matt. 6:33). The calling is to a trust in the Father and simplicity of life that does make us free. And I hear those words coming to me as a gracious invitation. Here is the way I heard them recently:

> I was invited out to a college to speak the other day—
>> you always want to do your best at a college.
> They are such reservoirs of knowledge and erudition—
>> at least it seems they certainly should be
>> when one considers how much learning
>> the freshmen bring with them and
>> how little the seniors actually take away.
> There was also the added disadvantage of
>> being in my own hometown—
> Five hundred miles is about the distance at which I begin
>> to change into a downright expert on any number of
>> important topics and subjects.
>
> So I had studied hard—and prayed earnestly—for seriously,
>> it is a deep challenge to speak to people that age.
> To try to add some direction to them from out
>> here where I am—
>> these thirty-odd years from commencement.
> And to try to do so in a way that will not tarnish
>> the brightness of their optimism.
>> It is not a task that I take lightly.
>
> And I put on my best three-piece navy pinstriped suit—
>> thinking maybe I would at least look like
>> "a wise man from the east."
>> And I went out to chapel and spoke.
> They were courteous and they listened attentively to me.
>> Afterward I was down talking to some students—
>> I wasn't mobbed or anything like that—
>> my safety was never endangered.

When someone looked down at my suit and said,
    "Well look at that."
And I looked down to see what that was—
only to see that my vest was buttoned wrong.

All the time I had been standing in front of those students
    not to mention the faculty and the administration
    thinking I was looking reasonably important.
And all the time they must have been sitting there thinking
    where did they get this guy
    who doesn't even know how to button his clothes?

Since it happened—let me try to salvage
    a bit of my wounded pride and honor
    by philosophizing about it for a moment or two.
It is not hard to button your vest wrong you know—
all you have to do is put the second button in the top hole.
    Or else slip the second hole over the top button.
    From then on it is as easy as falling off a log.
Because the rest will follow along slick as a whistle—
    all you have to do is start wrong—
    ending wrong will take care of itself.

And do you know how I hear the words of Christ
    coming to me these days?
    Very simply.
    I guess they would have to be for a
    fifty-four-year-old who hasn't passed buttoning yet.
But I hear him saying to me
    There is just one way to button your vest right.
    There is just one place to begin your life.
    There will always be a button left over
    or an extra hole—
    when you start wrong.
But if you begin right, if you seek first the kingdom
    and his righteousness—
the Father and I will guarantee that the rest will find
    their rightful places.

If I could have told them anything that morning—
    I mean in a way that it really stayed with them
    I guess it would have been about
        the place to start.
I don't know if they heard my words that morning,
    I just hope they heard my vest.[6]

I think at this juncture in my life I am becoming more and more aware that I am not smart enough to make all the decisions I must make. Neither am I strong enough to do all the things I should be doing. I'm not nearly wise enough to properly choose the path through the myriad ways that life can go wrong. So it comes as deep consolation and comfort to me to know that if I will begin right, if I will live in the Spirit, if I will seek to be like him, he will see to the endings.

What a calling it is! A calling to be finished and done with impurity, greed, hatred, jealousy, selfish ambition, and envy— to name a few of the things Paul lists as marks of being "like them." His call to love, joy, peace, patience, kindness, goodness, faithfulness, gentleness, and self-control.

Have you ever felt you should be true? Have you ever been impressed to be faithful? Have you known you should be honest? Have you ever wanted to know joy? Have you ever desired goodness, or wanted to live in peace? Have you ever wished that you were loving, and patient, and kind?

Then you have heard his voice. From deep within, he was calling you to be free.

8

Family Life Is a
Set of Givens

". . . as members of one body you were called . . ."

COLOSSIANS 3:15

Nobody, however, has lost the need for what a friend of mine calls "implicitness"—literally and figuratively, a place where, as the poet has it, when you go there they have to let you in, and where at the very least you can waken without surprise.

JANE HOWARD[1]

8
Family Life Is a Set of Givens

Some people don't have many heroes. I think some don't have any at all. The reason I think this is because every once and a while someone tries to treat me like I'm one. It is bad enough when you are by yourself about a thousand miles from home. But it's terrible when your family happens to be there when one of these hero-starved people happens to think you might be one. I was walking through a lobby with Peg and Leigh at a Praise Gathering when this lady came up to me and said, "Bob Benson! Can I just touch you?" I wish she hadn't said that. I must have heard it a hundred times since then around the house. Mostly when I am getting "uppity" about something one of the family will say, "Bob Benson! Can I just touch you?" And I have to explain to them that we gospel heroes just can't go around letting everybody touch us.

Seriously, I'm scared when I think about going to some place and talking to the same group of people five or six times. And know that they are going to sit there and listen to me expectantly with all kind of needs and hurts and dreams poking around inside them. It helps to start right in telling them that

125

God has something to to say to them. I want them to believe it. And I want them to listen for his voice.

I am not sure just when or even how I arrived at this conclusion—and it has helped to read it stated so tersely by Rabbi Heschel. "Preach in order to pray. Preach in order to inspire others to pray. The true test of a sermon is that it can be converted to prayer."[2] For a long time now I have felt that when I finished speaking there should be some time of guided or private prayer during which the people present could themselves speak to God. What they have to say to him may be in connection with what I have been discussing—or it may be a thousand miles from my topic. But I want them to have some time to listen and to respond to the calling voice of God before we dismiss and go our separate ways.

One of the ways I sometimes try to get them to participate in this prayer service is to ask them to put their hand on the shoulder of the person sitting next to them. When they all cooperate everyone is both touching someone and being touched by someone else. Then I ask them to bow their heads and close their eyes and join me in an exercise of prayer about being members of the body of Christ.

First, I want them to feel the hand that is resting on them. I sometimes instruct everyone to give a little pat on the shoulder so that they all will be aware of the hand reaching out to touch them. I say everyone. There are always some people who are reluctant to touch the person next to them, especially if they are strangers. And the ranks of the reluctant often swell when I get to the patting part. But most of the people will do it even if they grin nervously to assure their neighbor that this was not their idea. I want each person present to sense a hand touching them. Then I want them to believe that the hand resting on their shoulder is truly the hand of God reached out to them through the body of Christ.

It is a beautiful thing to behold as people begin to realize that they are not alone. They are members of a body—the body of Christ. I ask them to take some time to give thanks for all that being members of the body has meant to them over the years. I can imagine what is going on in their hearts. For I am mindful that most of us would never have made it, had it not been for the love and the prayers of those who have been the hand of

God reaching out to us as the body of Christ. Nearly always the place where we are meeting is filled with the sweet sound and aroma of praise as the people meditate during this part of the prayer exercise.

There is also another response that I want people to make after they have expressed their gratitude for the blessings of life in the body. I want each one to become aware of the shoulder on which their hand is laid. I want each one to consider the other thing it means to be a part of the body. Are their hands really saying to their neighbor in the pew, this hand will paint your house, this hand will cook the meals while your husband is in the hospital, this hand will reach into its own pocket and freely share everything there is as long as there is anything at all to divide? Are they willing for their hand to be the open, helping, suffering hand of God stretched out as a part of the body of Christ to others?

A Community of Believers

I like this prayer ceremony because it seems to help people see the lovely duality that exists in the body of Christ. For "body" is a unique metaphor. It is one that shows us that we are receiving life even as we are to be giving it, that we are being nurtured even as we are to be nurturing, that we are healing even as we are being healed.

It is true that the calling of God to us is personal. And it is true that the call comes to us in the depths of our own hearts. It is sounded into our own personality, background, and present experience. It is authentically ours. But it is most often heard in the midst of the body. And it is lived out in the community of believers. It is understood and affirmed and believed by the body together. It is undertaken and conserved with the mutual love and strength of the group.

I think it is because of the deep importance of body-life that so much of the teachings of the Epistles in the New Testament are given over to how we are to live with each other. Sometimes it seems that little is mentioned about winning the lost. It is as if the writers believed that if we could learn to be to each other all that we were supposed to be, the lessons we had learned in awareness and compassion would issue forth in all of the arenas of our lives. And that would in turn attract and compel those who do not know the Christ whose body we form.

And so it is here in in this particular place in Colossians that Paul reminds us that we are called in one body, and he describes how the members of the body should treat each other.

Bill Cosby has a funny little routine he does on jogging. He relates that since everybody else was jogging and talking about it he would give it a try. I don't think he made a habit of it because he said he was buying a very expensive set of running shoes that jog by themselves. But he did set his clock for 5:30 one morning and when the alarm went off he swung his legs off the edge of the bed and sat there in the "dawn's early light." His legs said, "What is going on?" To which he replied, "We are going jogging." "Jogging? What on earth for?" his legs mumbled. And Bill answered, "Because we have overeaten." And his legs commented, as they were crawling back under the covers, "Let the mouth and the stomach go jogging, we're going back to bed."

With his special perception Bill reminds us that as the body, we have not only unique privileges, but we have equally deep responsibilities. There is an interconnectedness about us. And the whole body must do whatever one part of the body undertakes to do. It should not be an unheeded example to those of us who are members of the body of Christ.

Affirmation for Highest Dreams

One of the first things Paul suggests is that being members of the body should change the way we see each other. He reminds us to take notice that we are all ". . . God's chosen people, holy and dearly loved . . ." (Col. 3:12).

If we could really begin to believe this it would change the way we look at one another. Or perhaps if we would change the way we look at each other we could begin to believe it. It is either one way or the other. Or both. It seems that most of the problems we have with one another begin in all the things we fail to see in each other.

Rabbi Heschel tells us that "awe is a way of being in rapport with the mystery of all reality. The awe that we sense or ought to sense when standing in the presence of a human being is a moment of intuition for the likeness of God which is concealed in his being."[3]

We usually make our first judgments about people on the basis of what we can see with our eyes. And, as Leo Buscaglia says, "the eye is really the most inaccurate, the most inconsistent, and the most prejudicial organ we have in the body."[4] We are so quick to see that other persons are too fat or too thin or too ugly or too short. So on the basis of looks, size, posture, a double knit leisure suit or something just about as essential to what a person really is, we form an opinion which we resolutely resist changing from then on. And we fail to even notice, or remember, that before us is standing a person the Father has created in his own image and into whom he has placed his kind and loving gifts.

We need to cultivate a habit so beautifully described by Virginia Stem Owens in her book, *And The Trees Clap Their Hands:*

> I look around me at the people gathered unwittingly with me for this sacrament at Sambo's. . . . Perhaps these strangers don't know . . . that a sacrifice at the center of the world upholds their life. Perhaps they don't know that their hands are holy and are holding holy things. . . . But for me, for a moment at least, there is an extraordinary sweetness in these faces. The light breaks across them, they lift and turn, call to one another. . . . Even should they not know and bless the Life that is in them or confess whose it is, it knows and blesses them. It winks at me slyly from their unsuspecting faces, bounds outside to the last shred of cloud, and slouches past the window again, disguised as an indifferent afternoon paper boy.[5]

I am convinced that marvelous things would begin to happen to each one of us in the body if we could all begin to see each other like this. I think more of us would be standing on our tiptoes reaching for the stars if we suddenly realized that everybody else had just been waiting for us to begin.

One of the big words in the vocabulary of the church these days is "ministry." Churches are known by the number and the variety of their "ministries." There are ministries to children, to singles, to youth, to senior citizens and to any other age group sufficiently large enough to merit the interest and attention of a staff member. There are prayer ministries, cassette ministries, bus ministries, clothing ministries and jail ministries. Almost any activity of the church that is undertaken is listed and described as one of the "ministries." And the more the better, of course. "A full service bank" is an expression the banking industry uses to describe the activities of one of its members. And a "full service church" in our society is a church that has "ministries" for everybody.

Ministry is usually thought about as something we do for someone else. That is certainly one of the ideas suggested by Jesus in his use of the metaphors "salt" and "light" in the Sermon on the Mount. His very choice of these two everyday illustrations shows his deep insight into the plight of mankind. The world, he indicates by his choice of remedies, has at least two fatal flaws.

The first is a constant tendency to deteriorate. It cannot seem to stop itself from going bad. Society always seems to need a preservative minority to prevent its decay. And his second insight is that the world is a very dark place to live. Some external light is needed to bring brightness to a society that has little or no light of its own.

Both history and the morning newspaper relentlessly remind us of the accuracy of the observations of Jesus. It does not take much of a threat to any of us—to our systems, our entitlements, our rights, or our places in line—to change us into angry, violent people. Lewis Thomas, medical administrator, researcher, and writer, notes with his usual keen insight into us all, "Our behavior toward each other is the strangest, most unpredictable, and unaccountable of all the phenomena with which we are obliged to live. In all of nature, there is nothing so threatening to humanity as humanity itself."[6]

A man in our community was recently convicted of the shotgun slaying of a policeman, a young man who was a husband and a father. The man was sentenced to life imprisonment. By all accounts he was a fairly decent man who had never been in much trouble. On the television screen in our living room he looked about like one of the rest of us. But under some pressures of a particular moment in a set of circumstances that were evidently intolerable to him, decay and darkness overtook him. And neither he, nor his family, nor the family of the dead man will ever be completely whole in the sunshine again.

And so the story goes. People are never far from deteriorating into something less than they imagined they were, and they are always slipping into some dark deed that was beneath anything they ever figured they would be capable of doing.

Jesus looked at this world and described it accurately. He hurt for this world for which he had come to die. And he prescribed a remedy for it. He said it needed salt to preserve it and light to illuminate it. And it is satisfying to think that we are the agents who are helping to keep the world from decay and darkness.

But there is something else sounding out to me from these words about salt and light and about ministry. This other idea, faintly disturbing, is beginning to redefine the word "ministry" for me. Maybe it is not always some act or deed that passes virtue, goodness and strength from those of us who are so lavishly endowed with these qualities to those less fortunate who would have had to do without if we had not come along as "ministers."

Henri J. M. Nouwen, in his journal published under the title, *Gracias*, gives us a new definition. The journal grew out of the better part of a year which he spent in South America. It was a time of personal searching for direction for his own life—life which the rest of us would already deem both useful and filled with ministry. He wrote that he was ". . . beginning to conclude that true liberation is freeing people from the bonds that have prevented them from giving their gifts to others."[7]

Could it have been that Jesus is calling us to be salt so that we would be seasoning to each other? A kind of a quality which will release and enhance all that which had long ago been stored deep inside by God himself? We don't put salt on green beans because we like the taste of salt, you know. We do it because it makes them taste more like what a green bean ought to taste like. Then we can say, "Now those are green beans."

And could it be that Jesus is calling us to shine light into the darkness so that whatever it is that God had placed there will be brightly illuminated? Is he asking us to bring light that is both healing and enhancing to the long-obscured works of his Father in the hearts and lives of others?

It seems to me that it is very likely the true essence of ministry has more to do with *being* to another than with some act or deed which we have come to believe we must be *doing* to, for, or on them. Perhaps the deepest, kindest thing we can do for anyone is to just be there for them in such a way that all they are and all the gifts they possess will be released and affirmed.

If this is true, it will probably begin to come about as we learn to perceive each other as Paul has suggested. Perhaps that's why he reminds us in this passage that we are all "God's chosen people, holy and dearly beloved."

Everybody needs and deserves to be surrounded with belief and affirmation that will form a pad from which their hopes and dreams and gifts can be launched. This is at least part of the reason, I think, that Paul tells us we are "called as members of one body." It is in the body of Christ that we are supposed to be surrounded with this seasoning, healing, enhancing love and care.

We all know how very much it means to be believed in. Leo Buscaglia, in his thought-provoking book, *Living, Loving, Learning* reminded me again of "Pygmalion in the Classroom," a study done by a group of researchers from Harvard. They would go to elementary school teachers at the beginning of the school year and tell them that they had designed a test which could prove most helpful to them. The results would correctly predict which students were going to grow intellectually during the coming school year. Leo called it "The Harvard Test of Intellectual Spurts" because he said it told which students were going to "spurt" that year. The educators promised it would pick out the right students and it was very, very accurate.

Given permission to give the test, unbeknownst to the teacher, they administered an old, obsolete I.Q. test. When the students had finished the test, the papers were collected and the researchers threw them in the wastebasket. Then they picked five names at random from the rollbook and sat down with the teacher and said, "Now these are the students in your class who are going to have a very good year. Watch these kids. One of them is Rachel Smith," they informed the teacher. "Rachel Smith?" the teacher replied incredously, "She wouldn't 'spurt' if you shot her from a cannon. I have had two of her brothers and each one of the Smiths is dumber than the last." But the educators maintained that the test hardly ever was wrong in its findings and that Rachel's progress in the ensuing year could be readily observed.

You can imagine what happened that semester, can't you? Yes, you can. Rachel never had a chance to be her same old self. Under a barrage of "Rachel, would you write this on the board this morning," "Rachel will lead the line to the lunch room today," "Is that a new dress, Rachel? It sure is pretty," "Thank you, Rachel, that was very good," Rachel 'spurted' all over the place. And so did every name they put on that list.[8]

Paul is saying here that everyone of our names belong on the list. We are all "God's chosen people, holy and dearly loved." I think one of my all-time favorite quotes is from a little boy in elementary school who said, "My teacher thought I was smarter than I wuz. So I wuz!" And all of us need to be in a body that believes we are smarter and better and more gifted than we have ever dared to think we were. For this is one of the ways that each of us will begin to hear the calling voice of God.

One of the things that the hand on our shoulder in the prayer exercise is saying to us is a deep, affirmative, "I believe in you." And our hand should be saying to the one whose shoulder we are touching, "I believe in who you are and what you can become because of the gifts that God has put within you." For every now and then (preferably now), we all need someone to come to us and say, "Well done," or "You're the most," or "That is just great!" Or to use a phrase my kids are using a lot these days, although not very often about their dad, "You're awesome."

Forgiveness for Darkest Deeds

At the same time Paul tells us that we are all "holy and dearly loved" and that we should be conducting ourselves toward each other as if we were, he is also busy being a realist about life among the members of the body. He gives the admonition to "bear with each other and forgive whatever grievances you may have against one another. Forgive as the Lord forgave you" (Col. 3:13).

Even though we are a body of people who are called to great things—a body that is given diverse and wonderful gifts—it is still true, sooner or later (and too many times it is sooner) one of us goes out and does something that is just really dumb. We knew it was dumb when we were doing it and that just made it all the dumber. And all of the sudden the community which hopefully had been going about its work of affirmation is called on to do some bearing and some forgiving.

In a lot of the places I go, I find that people love singing songs like, "I'm so glad I'm a part of the family of God," and "We're part of the family that's been born again." You can start one of these songs and everybody will just join right in with great joy and conviction. Well, part of being "part of the family" often demands what Jane Howard calls "dealing with direness." In her book, Families, she lists ten earmarks of a good family. And number five, right in the middle of the list, is the requirement that good families "deal squarely with direness." She writes:

> Pity the tribe that doesn't have, and cherish, at least one flamboyant eccentric. Pity too the one that supposes it can avoid for long the woes to which all flesh is heir. Lunacy, bankruptcy, suicide and other unthinkable fates sooner or later afflict the noblest of clans with an undertow of gloom. Family life is a set of givens, someone once told me, and it takes courage to see certain givens as blessings rather than as curses. Contradictions and inconsistencies are givens, too.[9]

Upon his retirement, my father undertook to compile a family history of the Bensons. Like everything he decides to do, he did it methodically and well. He has always been very proud of his father and mother and wanted to know more about his ancestors. His own father and his paternal grandfather were both good businessmen and devout churchmen. Proceeding down the trunk and out on some of the limbs of his family tree, my dad made some interesting discoveries.

He traced us back up into east Tennessee into Smith County around Carthage. Such a search takes you to the courthouse for deeds and titles of properties bought and sold. Unfortunately, the first Benson up there that my father could tie us all to must have been very poor. At least, according to the courthouse records, he never owned any land. Furthermore, there was a ferry up at Carthage that ran back and forth across the Cumberland River which cost a nickel to ride. And you had to sign the register when you rode it. Evidently old John R. didn't have a nickel because he doesn't show up in the records as ever having made the trip. Fortunately for our family pride, things have been more impressive since we moved to town.

For a long time Dad didn't think too much about Mom's side of the tree. She was from Alabama and I'm not sure he thought they had family trees down there. But he decided that his children would also be interested in their mother's people and he persuaded Mom to do some research on her ancestors. She keeps finding all kind of landowners right on back to William Penn. It discouraged my father a little, I think.

If you keep poking around in family trees you will have to "deal with some direness." One of my uncles was rather famous and once was greeted with a parade upon his return from New York. Unfortunately, the records show he was returning from an extended stay in prison at Sing Sing.

It is not very much different in the "family of God." The body of Christ is always having to learn to deal with something that one of us has gone out and done—or maybe it was one of our children or one of our children's children. But the question of "direness" is nearly always with us.

We are not always so good at dealing with it, either. One summer Sunday morning, our family decided to visit the services of a church about which we had heard a lot of good things. The pastor happened to be preaching that day on the matter of disciplining errant members of the congregation. He was contending for the right of the elders to deal with such matters as might arise. He was also reminding the elders of the sacred responsibilities and duties involved even in potentially painful situations. Although we were only visitors, he was contending and reminding so earnestly that we could not help but suspect there were some matters that had already come up. He offered as evidence for his sermon some paragraphs from the constitution of his particular denomination. The official rules stated that in any such circumstances there were three factors to be considered. The three points themselves were not necessarily surprising. But the order of importance which they were given was mildly disturbing to me, to say the least.

First, in all matters, God was to be glorified. Certainly it seemed this should be the first priority of the church. It was the order of the next two propositions which disturbed me. Secondly, the pastor went on to say, the body was to protect its own purity. Finally, the errant member was to be ministered to. I wasn't sure that point numbers two and three were in the proper order. I'm still not.

Forgiveness isn't much of a trick if everybody is glorifying God. And it isn't too difficult if nobody is doing anything to embarrass or discredit the rest of us. Where it really gets to be a chore is when someone goes out and does something dumb. In fact, that's the problem with the whole matter of forgiveness. There is always this relationship between the senselessness of the deed itself and the depth of the need for forgiveness. The darker the deed, the deeper the necessity for the healing balm of mercy. Burying the wounded so the rest of us will be healthy doesn't seem like much of a way to build the army.

Some time ago on the radio I heard a song that I liked. The lyrics were talking about a place where:

> everybody knows your name,
> and they're always glad you came.

Somebody told me that it was the theme song for a television program about a saloon. I still wish they'd been singing it about the church.

In the *Reader's Digest* some time ago, there was a little paragraph about a Sunday school class that was searching for a name. It was a class of people who had been drawn together mostly because they were all filled with the same kind of hurts and needs and dreams. There were lots of suggestions for a name given but one was chosen because it seemed to say what everybody wanted it to say about them. It was "The Come Just As You Are Class." I think I would have voted for it too.

There is some keen insight into the gospel in that name. Those people were looking for a name which best described what was unique to them as a class. They must have decided that the strongest bond holding them together was not one of their strengths—it was their weaknesses that made them one.

If the word gets around that they are really living up to their name it may create a problem, because somebody is going to "come just as they are." And some time in the future the name might have to be discreetly changed to something like "Come Just As We Are."

More and more I am coming to believe that the body is bound together by its weaknesses. Perhaps before we can begin to affirm others in their gifts, we will have to accept them and forgive them because they are weak as we are weak.

There was a deep spirit of forgiveness and acceptance among the people who were up at Homecoming, the retreat where we built the altar. I think it began with something which was done at registration—under some mild protests and questioning I might add. "Do I have to?" and "what are these for?" were the two most often asked questions. There was a reason for making an instant photo of everyone as they signed in at the lodge. "Just bring it along to the opening session," was the only instruction given as we were handed our picture mounted on a card.

There was one thing we wanted to try to begin the very first time we met. Retreats are alike in many ways. The first day and a half or so seems to be spent in trying to become a group. Usually this really begins to happen about midway through the final service and then everybody suddenly wonders why we had wasted all that time walking around like strangers. So we had planned to open up the retreat trying to get the "Sunday and good-by" feeling on a "Friday and hello" afternoon. And the ability of a group to become a community—or better still, "the body"—always seems to come in some direct proportion to the willingness that they have to give themselves to each other.

In many ways it would seem that this sense of belonging would be just what everybody is seeking and it would come about very naturally and very quickly. But the truth is most of us go along through life with enough masks in our luggage to keep ourselves cleverly disguised in almost any situation, including retreats. And it is difficult to share ourselves with a new circle of people.

Certainly we don't want people to know the worst about us. But, paradoxically, it is only those who know the worst about us and still believe in us anyway that we really trust. And it is not just the worst that we hide either, we are afraid to reveal our best as well. We are very careful with our "I really do like you's" and our "I care about you's." So carefully hiding our worst and cautiously guarding our best, we try to build some new community on the safe middle ground of anonymity. Ralph Keyes, in a fine book on community entitled *We, the*

Lonely People, writes," . . . I guess that's the main thing I've learned about our quest for community—that the key thing keeping us apart is our fear . . . especially of each other . . . . Once someone, once I, can take the risk, break the ice, and say how I really feel, it's always amazing how many others turn out just to have been waiting their turn. Then the community begins . . . . But to join that community, each one of us must take that hard, terrifying first step—saying—even to one person—'I need you.' "10

It was our hope that the picture on the card would be both a symbol and a way of our giving ourselves to each other. During the first session, there were admonitions made about openness being the key to community and community being the key to any kind of life-changing process. Nearly always what happens to us from above is conditioned by what is going on between us.

So there was a time for each of us to write about ourselves on the card under the picture. Things like who we were, what we were hoping for, our defeats, our successes, what it was that made us sing and what it was that made us sad. We were to write as much as we were willing to let the others know about us. It was a quiet, solemn time when the only sounds you could hear were pen and pencil points scratching across cards in our laps as we reduced the whole of our experiences to the series of marks, slashes, dots, and scribblings that would let other people into our hearts.

When we finished writing, and if we were willing to trust the rest of the group with the person we had described on the card, we placed it in a basket at the front of the room. The basket was going to be put at the entrance to the prayer chapel. Then, as the people went in to pray they would take a card with them to the altar and make that person a matter of special prayer and concern. On the last day we all took a card from the basket to take home with us and made a covenant to continue to remember the person pictured and described for the coming year.

The picture cards came to give us all a sense of belonging to each other. Each time we went to the chapel we felt we were meeting someone in a new way. We also realized that we, too, were being picked out of the basket and someone was looking at our faces and reading our scribblings and praying for us and for the things we had been willing to confide to the community. We began to be bound up together as we saw, and were seen, in the light of our hopes and our dreams—and in our heartaches and struggles.

One afternoon, my son Robert was standing in the back of the chapel and he noticed more than one person digging through the pictures in the basket. He later said he thought to himself that it was not quite fair for a person to read through all the cards if they were not going to take them inside to pray over them. Then he realized the people were looking for their own cards. Evidently there were some things they wished to add— some things they would like for the "body" to know and care about. They had come to believe they could trust the rest of us. There did indeed seem to be a reservoir of acceptance and love turned loose among us. It was opened because we were willing to be bound together by our weakness, and because out of our weakness there came strength.

Again I would remind you that Paul tells us that we are "called as members of one body." In the body there is to be found affirmation of our strengths and acceptance of our weaknesses. And "living in the body" is a metaphor that has very wonderful dimensions to it.

It is like the picture portrayed by the people in the prayer service with their hands on each other's shoulders. Even as our hand reaches out to touch someone else we are being touched. Ministering, we are ministered to. Giving, we are given unto. Lifting, we are lifted up. Saddened, we are made glad.

In our church we used to sing the old song:

> He loves me, He loves me
> He loves me this I know.
> He gave Himself to die for me,
> Because He loves me so.

And I still like to sing it, because I still believe it. But I am thinking these days that Kurt Kaiser was closer to the deep intentions of God when he wrote this song for us to sing:

> O how He loves you and me,
> O how He loves you and me:
> He gave His life, what more could He give:
> O how He loves you, O how he loves me,
> O how he loves you and me.[11]

For the calling of God comes to us in community. We are called in one body.

9

When the Mind Is Made Up

". . . to win the prize for which God has called me heavenward in Christ Jesus."

PHILIPPIANS 3:14

In the camp this meant committing my verse—many thousands of lines to memory. To help me with this I improvised decimal counting beads and, in transit prisons, broke up matchsticks and used the fragments as tallies. . . .
My memory found room for them! It worked. But more and more of my time—in the end as much as one week every month—went into the regular repetition of all I had memorized.

ALEKSANDR I. SOLZHENITSYN[1]

9
When the Mind Is Made Up

In the mid-thirties, my dad realized that the little house in McClurkan was not going to be big enough to hold his rapidly expanding family. So he bought some property east of Nashville on Brush Hill Road. He had spent summers and weekends nearby as he was growing up, for the property was only a mile or so down the road from Grandfather and Grandmother Benson's summer cottages on the river bluff in Haysboro. For many years they had escaped there on weekends from the heat and the noise of the city.

In 1937, we all moved into a brand new home at 3622 Brush Hill Road. The house sat just about in the middle of the four acres Dad had purchased. The front yard was nearly level, and had five or six magnificent old hackberry trees that provided shade in the summer, limbs for swings and climbing, and plenty of ammunition for the blowguns we made out of cane. Just behind the house, the lot rolled down a hillside into a little valley with a creek which roughly formed the boundary line. The bottom, as we called it, also had some great trees in it, including elms, black walnuts, and sycamores. There was a spring under the side of the hill which flowed cold and clear all year round. It was a marvelous place for a boy to grow up.

Our new home was just about at the edge of the suburbs on that side of Nashville at the time. However, progress was on the way and it wasn't long before they built the Dan Mills Elementary School about four blocks from our house. It was closer than that if you cut through Mack Parsons' and Harold Conn's backyards—which was what I did when I walked, because farther on up Riverwood some people named Bradley had about the meanest chow dog I had ever seen. With the exception of Jack Allen's pet turkey, which roamed all over his yard, it was by far the meanest creature in the neighborhood.

My brother John and I were at school that first day it opened. Until John moved to Hendersonville and his daughter Ann changed schools there had been a Benson in Dan Mills Elementary for nearly thirty years. It was a steady, reliable part of the community. Eloise Watkins Fry, the new young principal on opening day, along with some seasoned teachers like Miss Catherine, Mrs. Hall, Miss Dickinson, and Mrs. McDaniels, spent the rest of their careers there.

Our neighborhood was out past the ends of both the Porter Road and Inglewood bus lines which reached out in an easterly direction from downtown. There was a shuttle bus that ran back and forth between the two lines. Winding back and forth through the neighborhoods it made its journey up Riverside Drive, which we always called Double Drive because it was a World War I Memorial. The lanes were separated by a grassy bank which was planted with iris and shrubs like lilac bushes. It went nearly into town before it ducked under railroad tracks as it turned into Shelby Park. The bus route crossed over the tracks at Greenwood where it picked up Double Drive to McGavock Pike and down big Riverwood hill.

The hill was the scene of many happy sleigh rides in the winters when we were fortunate enough to have snow. It was also the scene of great tragedy when my cousin, John Aughey, was killed in an auto accident with some of his friends in a crash against a great old tree in the curve near the bottom. Next came Brush Hill, and it was a short trip the rest of the way through Haysboro to Gallatin Pike.

Of course, if we missed the bus going in that direction, we could ride it back the other way, and connect with the Porter Road bus—if we hadn't lost our properly punched orange transfer slip.

The buses were big, old, lumbering affairs that smoked and fumed and were cold in the winter and hot in the summer. The Southern Coach Lines, the forerunner to the Metro Transit Authority, must have had the world's largest collection of ancient conveyances. The shuttle buses were usually even older.

The trip back and forth to town usually involved some waiting at the end of the line for the connection, whether one did it loitering in the drugstore at the end of the old Porter Road carline or over on Gallatin Pike at Tom Perryman's ESSO Station. When the bus did come, there was still some waiting to do while the driver checked his watch, punched a new set of transfer slips, rolled nickels and dimes from the farebox, and cranked up the new destination on the front of the bus for the trip back toward town.

One of those inbound destination signs used to be ST CECILIA. Since I always got off when the bus got to town, I never was quite sure where I would have been if I had ridden on to St. Cecilia. Later on, when I was old enough to drive and began to cruise around the town in Mom's old '37 Ford, I discovered that St. Cecilia was a Catholic Convent out at the end of Eighth Avenue where the road turned north to go around the hill to Bordeaux and on to Clarksville, Tennessee and Hopkinsville, Kentucky.

Even then Catholicism was sort of remote to me since my contact with Catholics was minimal. The first Catholic I knew was a kid named Joe Brown, who was tough as nails. We all played football in the field up by Roland Downing's house, and I soon learned to stay out of his way. The only other thing I knew was that he did not go to Dan Mills. He went to a Catholic school called Holy Name. The way he played football "Holy Terror" on his jersey would have been more appropriate. Unfortunately, my only other reference point for Catholics came from our pastor, who would occasionally refer to them obliquely when he was preaching on the dangers of being unequally yoked with unbelievers.

Some twenty-five or so years later, St. Cecilia was to become a kind of milepost in my life as I passed her every morning on my way up the ramp and down the hill into MetroCenter to the new building that housed the Benson Company. By this time, she had acquired some snazzy new neighbors, including the spanking new Maxwell House Hotel (this was a hostelry name long famous in Nashville from its old location at Fourth and Church for being the site of my high school Junior Class Banquet and other significant bits of local and American history). But I still did not know much about St. Cecilia.

Not too long ago, our local paper carried a lovely story entitled "The Brides of Christ," and I learned about the 125 or so sisters who live there on that hill overlooking North Nashville. St. Cecilia is a great red brick Victorian building that has been kind enough to lend her name to Southern Coach Lines for a bus route. The article was very perceptive and informative and its writer/photographer did a thorough job of filling in the gaps in my long-neglected knowledge about St. Cecilia.

The thing that was almost immediately apparent was that amidst all the changes in the bus lines, the neighborhood, the Maxwell House, my life and almost everything and everybody else, St. Cecilia had remained remarkably the same as she was when she had been founded more than 120 years ago on the very same spot. Although it had taken me 50 years or so to learn about her, the story would have been the same no matter when I got around to hearing it. I think that it interested me because St. Cecilia had remained unchanged over all those years. Her ability to remain exactly what she had started out to be was intriguing to me.

The way of life there is ordered and regulated and endures as the years go by, as the sisters seek first to become spiritually perfect and saints of God. After this primary goal, their lives are given to winning others to Christ through their apostolate or job. The sisters there belong to the Dominican order founded in France in the thirteenth century, and their apostolate is teaching. Everyone in the convent either teaches or has a job that supports the teachers.

Each year a handful of young women come to the convent to give up their life in the world around them and take the vows of poverty, chastity and obedience. Although they are average, normal, attractive, and enthusiastic, they bid farewell to their family and friends to begin the lengthy process by which they will become sisters. It is a rigorous period that can last from two to nine years. The first few years are spent in a new life made up of prayer, worship, silence, study and play. At the end of this time, known as the foundation, they will write their final vows to Christ. In a public ceremony that family and friends may witness, each one signs the vows in her own handwriting. The vows are then put in the archives of the convent.

The newspaper story told about the death of Sister Henry Suso. She had entered the convent in 1937 when she was just seventeen years old. Two years later she had taken the vows and for the next forty-three years she led the life of a "religious" in total commitment to God and to her apostolate of teaching. She taught in various parochial schools and had served for a decade as president of Aquinas Junior College. In 1977 she had been named principal of St. Gertrude School in Cincinnati. She held that position until she was forced by cancer to return to the convent in January of 1982. Although her last few months were spent in pain, her illness did not seem to affect her spirit. She confided to her friends, "It could be that God will let me get well and I'll go back to work. Or it could be that this is the end. Either way, it will be God's will. I can't lose, for I'll either be working for him on earth, or else I'll be in heaven."

She died on May 27th of that year. It was the task of the prioress general of the convent to retrieve from the archives the vows she had written out by hand at age nineteen. They were placed in Sister Henry's hands to be buried with her. It was a moving thing to me to think about a young person writing vows to God and then proceeding to live them out resolutely and steadfastly. And then, after having lived those promises for a lifetime, that one would lay quietly before him with those same unbroken vows in her hands. What an inspiration, in death as in life, to present such faithfulness as a gift to God.

Time will probably go right on changing things: North Nashville, MetroCenter, the hotel business and, I hope and fear, myself as well. But as long as there are people like Sister Henry who make vows and live up to them, it isn't likely that St. Cecilia will change very much. I wonder if some quality of permanence might not come to all of us if we, too, were to make

deep vows to God and remain faithful to them. I also wonder
that if it can happen in a convent, might it not also occur wherever people make abiding commitments and then go forth to
carry them out in life and in death?

Commitments Are to Be Kept

Commitment is a religious word through and through. It
means a deposit committed to someone's trust. It is like entrust-
ing valuable papers or goods to someone else by placing them
in their care, confident that they will be safely kept. Sister
Henry, like all her sisters in Christ, was so convinced of the
trustworthiness of God himself that she committed herself to
him. Or as Paul put it, ". . . because I know whom I have
believed, and am convinced that he is able to guard what I have
entrusted (committed) to him for that day" (2 Tim. 1:12).

I keep running into this religious word, commitment, in
funny places. At least they seem funny to me—in novels and in
business magazines and in ads.

A while back, as a book club member who had failed to put
an "X" in the box marked "Send me no book at all this month"
I received in the mail the current dual selection for my very
own. One of the books was a novel, *Thy Brother's Wife.* I don't
generally read much fiction. (I have this feeling that the things
that are really happening are interesting enough.) Since it was
by Father Andrew M. Greeley I read some of the book. The
dust jacket said that Father Greeley was "one of the most influ-
ential thinkers in the world." Maybe it was my lack of awareness, but this fact seemed to be concealed from the readers of
the book fairly well.

The story seemed to have everything that stories are supposed to have these days. It reminded me of something Irvin S.
Cobb is quoted as saying, "I couldn't write the things they pub-
lish now, with no beginning and no end, and a little incest in the
middle."[2] As I made my way rather quickly to the last page, I
did read with some curiosity a brief statement at the end entitled, "A Personal Afterward." Greely was attempting to answer
a question that had also been vaguely forming in my mind
while reading the book. He wrote, "Why should a priest write a
novel, particularly a secular novel about adultery, incest, and

sacrilege? . . . This particular story will be successful if the reader is disconcerted by the tale of commitments that are imperfectly made and imperfectly kept—but still are kept."³ Since I was disconcerted by this, I suppose by the author's standards I would have to admit that the novel was a success.

But I didn't like the way he used the word. Even in a novel it seems that "commitment" is a word which should be describing something honored. Even when I don't keep my own commitments I think it might be better to change the word I use than it is to try to change the meaning of the word.

I came across the word again in an issue of *Fortune*.It was in an article about a West Coast company named Tandem Computers. The president, Jim Treybig, is almost messianic about what the article described as the Tandem gospel or management philosophy. The philosophy was built upon five precepts that were hardly novel. But Tandem's emphasis on them was a radical departure from most company's actual practices.

In talking about the company and its style, Treybig half-jokingly said, "I know this sounds like religion or something," adding, "It's almost like religion." A programmer with the company remarked, "I don't think someone who thought Tandem was just a job would work out, because Tandem expects commitment."

Then the word fairly jumped out at me from an ad run a few months ago in some leading business magazines. It was one of those four headline words in a campaign by the International Harvester Corporation to sell something to somebody. Reflecting on their company and the 150 years of business that had resulted in their truck and farm tractor divisions, they felt that their success was due to their devotion to the idea of being ready to "help whenever we can, wherever we can, however we can." Those are words that would stir the heart of any copywriter, and with the inspiration of a century and a half of such dedicated service the headline could only read, "The Commitment Is Forever." There wasn't any ad campaign a few months later to announce that, due to a lack of profitability, the tractor and farm equipment division had been sold to a competitor. So much for commitment. And for that matter, I guess so much for forever, too.

In all fairness though, it must be confessed that commitment is not a word which just troubles heros and heroines in would-be best-selling novels and companies who want to be the best or companies who are losing money selling tractors. It has been a tough word for real, live religious folk to get a handle on, as well.

I was driving over to Knoxville on Interstate 40 a summer or so ago. I was moving along with the traffic, trying to stay with a late model Pontiac with a radar detector that had passed me earlier. Of course, I am much too spiritual to own such a device myself. All of a sudden, almost out of nowhere, a young lady in a bright green Vega passed us like we were sitting still. Glancing at my own speedometer, I noted that I certainly was not sitting still. And I figured she must be doing at least eighty-five miles per hour, if not ninety. I just had time to read her two bumper stickers as she whizzed around me. The one on the left declared THIS DRIVER IS HIGH ON JESUS. We had a yellow Vega once (they insisted on making them in outlandishly bright colors), and on the basis of my experience with the one we had, I determined that what she was doing was hazardous to her health. I thought if she kept on going that fast in that old Vega she was going to be high somewhere—and soon.

The other sticker, misapplied to the trunk, proclaimed, I HAVE DECIDED TO FOLLOW JESUS. I didn't know how far behind him she thought she was that day, but it looked like she meant to catch up by the time she reached the Harriman Exit.

I'm not trying to say that I thought she was not committed because she was speeding. But I have seen many of us lots of times trying to catch up to our commitments. And it reminded me that there are some very good words for us in this moving passage in the third chapter of Philippians. It was the fervent prayer of Paul that he would "know Christ." If Paul had been a bumper sticker man I think his would have said, "I WANT TO KNOW CHRIST."

He was frank to say that he had not yet "attained . . . this" and that he had not "been made perfect." But he did tell us in words that speak of his deep intention to "win the prize for which God has called him heavenward in Christ Jesus." With a singleness of mind and an all-absorbing desire he had committed himself to cross the finish line. He was armed with a mind that was made up. "This one thing I do," was one of the great secrets of his life as an apostle.

A paragraph comes to mind from a little book that was given to me. The title of the book is *Letters to the Scattered Brotherhood*, and editor Mary Strong included the paragraph in this collection of letters of "genuine spiritual experience" by a variety of people she describes as having found "faith to walk in immortality now." It said, ". . . Much depends on making up your mind. The nature of the human animal, as you well know, is subject to suggestion. The feeling nature, when left to human devices is unprotected, easily dismayed, elated, bored, irritated. The mind is moved by noises, cold, heat, stupidities, a letter, the disloyalty of a friend. But when the mind is made up, all these challenges can be divinely met; you are not defenseless."[4]

In every area of life there are shining examples of people whose lives had such bright unity of purpose, a unity purchased at the cost of a great commitment. Such a person was Dag Hammarskjöld, the brilliant statesman who served his generation so well as Secretary-General of the United Nations. In 1961 he wrote in his journal: "I don't know Who—or what—put the question, I don't even know when it was put. I don't even remember answering. But at some moment I did answer YES to Someone—or Something—and from that hour I was certain that existence is meaningful and that, therefore, my life, in self surrender, had a goal." As early as age twenty he was able to write in his journal, "Ready at any moment to gather everything into one, simple sacrifice." So it is not surprising that in 1953 when he was elected to the high position his words were:

> For all that has been—Thanks
> To all that shall be—Yes![5]

Daily Deposits to Our Determination

It is obvious, however, that the total Christian life cannot be carried in the making of a single choice or decision. It would be much simpler if, as the poet said, we "could do some one great deed and die, and then rise triumphant into the sky." Instead, we are alternately driven from the right by wrong and lulled from the best by good. There are always shortcuts and bypasses and forks in the road. And it is as C. S. Lewis wrote in *Mere*

Christianity: ". . . every time you make a choice you are turning the central part of you, the part that chooses, into something a little different than what it was before. And taking your life as a whole, with all your innumerable choices, you are slowly turning this central thing either into a Heaven creature or into a hellish creature. . . ."[6]

Paul is telling us, though, that we can make a single choice around which all of the rest of our decisions can cluster and anchor themselves. People can choose how they will make their choices. This commitment to faithfulness, a mindset to persevere, is one true thing which we can do. We can make this determination, "I have started in one direction and I will steadfastly choose that which leads me forward toward the goal."

The foundation of my belief rests on the speaking voice of God. I did not call him. He had been and is calling me. The thesis of this book is that God has something to say to all of us. His words, coming to us in many ways and from many places, are always calling us to him. The commitment we must make is to listen.

The decision that is the most important matter in our lives has to do with our ability to hear him—to decide once and for all that every choice we make will be made in the light of its effect on our continued hearing of his voice calling to us. We must be always listening so that we may know Christ.

In the parable of the talents the master told the faithful servants that they would be put in charge of many things because they had been "faithful with a few things." Most often our great dream does not come to fruition because we were not "faithful" in the little daily dreams.

It is the daily deposits to our Christian commitment that begin to add up to riches in Christ. It is a series of small faithfulnesses. It is a sometimes barely noticed but continuing steadfastness. It is a pattern of habits, none of which may seem earthshaking in themselves, but which gradually provide the openings through which God comes to us. It is the sum total of these tiny, seemingly minor commitments that either erode and undercut or strengthen and fortify our "one great Yes!" When I think of how to describe this relationship of "our commitments" to "our commitment" I think of the words of Rabbi

Heschel, "Faith is the fruit of a seed planted in the depth of a lifetime."[7]

More than once I have heard people say, and the words are not foreign to my lips either, "I have tried to pray but I never seem to get any answer." The questions that immediately cause all of us who have said this to drop our heads and mumble our reply are questions like these, "How often did you pray?" "Over what period of time did you pray?" "How long would you be willing to continue to pray if it did not appear to you there had been answers?"

It is coming to me, belatedly I am afraid, that it is our responsibility to pray. And he has promised to speak to us so that we know we have been answered. I have never talked to anyone who said that they had been truly faithful in approaching God who did not also tell of his great faithfulness in coming to them with his presence and the answers. Jesus taught us the deep truth that if "we would pray in secret the Father would reward us openly."

Usually it is the same ones of us who speak of our prayer as being one-way conversations who also have been known to say, "I don't get anything out of reading the Bible." I think the same principles are in effect concerning the reading of the Word of God. Our call is to read the Word. He is the One who has promised that it will speak to us.

Probably in both the matters of prayer and Bible reading the thing about us through which we will begin to hear the answering voice of God is our faithfulness.

These things, prayer and Bible reading, are religious acts. It has been the contention of this book that the same diligence can be brought to every area of our lives and we will be able to hear him speaking to us. It lies in our simple acknowledgment or recognition that he is there and is earnestly seeking to communicate with us.

The Commitment Is to Listen

We were in Sunday school class recently, visiting before time for the lesson to start. In the informal setting we mingled with coffee, spiced tea and doughnuts, occasionally letting one eye drift down to read the name badge on a lapel. As we seated ourselves, greetings were extended to the visitors. Someone made announcements about upcoming activities including a Valentine banquet, and where and when to turn in the money.

Up to this point we could have been almost anybody, the PTA, the Kiwanis, the Rotary, Volunteer Firemen, or anyone of a thousand other groups or organizations. Coffee, name badges, comments on the weather, announcements and small talk catch just about everybody. Then a young singer, Billy Crockett, was introduced and he stood before us with his guitar. He asked us if we would sing with him before he sang for us and he softly led us:

"On a hill far away . . .
stood an old rugged cross . . ."

and then

"He leadeth me, oh blessed thought
O words with heavenly comfort fraught . . . ."

and next

"This is my Father's world
and to my listening ears . . . ."

and last

"Christ the Lord is risen today
A - - - - le - lu - jah . . ."

Suddenly we were not the PTA or the Rotary or Voluntary Firemen. We were worshipers. In our acknowledgment of him in a few verses of song each of us, in a way that was uniquely private and corporate, had heard the speaking voice of God.

One night recently we were coming to the end of a dinner party at our house. Peg had cooked a delicious meal and we had visited a long time in the living room afterward. We were all close friends and it seemed so good to have a quiet, unhurried time to be together. We laughed and talked and commiserated about our kids. Finally one couple said that they would have to be going and everybody else got up and put on their coats too. We were standing in the hall by the front door visiting for a final moment or two. Someone suggested we pray together before we parted. With bowed heads we lifted our hearts together to him and as we did the bonds of friendship slipped tighter around us all as we recognized the calling voice of him who makes us one.

I know it sounds better to sing when Billy Crockett plays his guitar. But you can hum a chorus or two of an old hymn to yourself in the car on the way to work. And I know it's easier to pray when you are in a circle of old friends with locked arms. But you can breathe a prayer in the elevator on the way to the dentist's office.

If you will acknowledge, recognize, hum, pray—if you will commit yourself to this process of listening—you will begin to realize that the voice you have heard so often across the days of your life has been his voice.

10

More Smiles
Than Faces

"The one who calls you is faithful and he will do it."

(Leo had advised a lady who was dying to visit some children in the hospital who were also dying.) Thank goodness she did. The wonder of wonders is that the children taught her to die. The minute she walked in, little kids went up to her and said, "Are you going to die, too?" . . . I don't know why, but she said, "Yes, I am!" A child said, "Are you afraid?" She said, "Yes." "Why are you afraid? You're gonna see God!" One little girl said, "Will you bring your doll?"

LEO BUSCAGLIA[1]

10
More Smiles Than Faces

I don't like good-bys.

I can't remember just how far back these feelings go, but I think they may have begun when I was seven or eight. Asthma was the culprit and the fall air was laden with football and falling leaves and asthma's accomplice, pollens. Once again breathing was so difficult for me that it was determined I needed the balmy, ocean breezes of Florida. This particular year Mom could not get away to go with me and, I am sure with some deep misgivings on the part of my parents, I was bundled up and sent off to Miami. I was to stay with some distant friends of my folks. I had never met the lady, her mother, or her teen-aged daughter, who were to be my family for some three months until Jack Frost and the winds of winter could cleanse the Tennessee air.

Some things about that fall are indelibly etched in my memory. I cannot forget the old house on N. W. 54th in Miami. It was not in very good shape because the hurricane of 1928 had severely damaged it, and since Mrs. Moore was a widow of limited means the repairs had been something less than extensive. I recall the flight down on the Eastern Airlines Silverliner with the glassine packet of airline stickers and postcards in the seat pocket in front of me. I remember Central Church of the Nazarene and Earlington Heights Elementary School, and riding my bicycle over to Alapattah Center. But mostly I remember being miserably and abjectly homesick. To this day, good-bys do not come easily to me.

So as I waited for my row to be called to board Republic 393 for Chicago one morning last fall I was engrossed in watching some rather tender and poignant farewells going on around me. And I observed more than one teary-eyed person looking forlornly at the giant bird outside the window that was in the process of gobbling up their loved ones. Since I was only going to Indiana for three days, I had managed to bear up as I had kissed my family good-by before leaving the house a little while before. I wondered, though, about the reasons and the lengths and the distances of some of the separations being dramatized before me in the waiting lounge at the Nashville airport.

Finally we were all on board, watching with rapt attention the demonstration of a series of procedures to be used in "unlikely events." I noted that the plane was largely filled with business types: salesmen, executives, and presidents of Amalgamated Widget Internationals. In the seat next to me a man armed with a handful of pencils and a calculator was already hard at work filling out expense reports and working out proposals. In front of me there was a man I figured was a real tycoon. I had seen him first in the terminal hard at work on the telephone up by Gate Sixteen and later in his temporary office with two brief cases and a secretary down at Gate Nineteen. He was a seasoned traveler, ignoring the row-by-row boarding sequence, and coming on almost last. He had walked up the aisle as if he had come on board to buy the plane or maybe even the airline. His secretary didn't have quite the same air of assurance as he did, but then she was carrying the two brief cases, a box, a newspaper, two coats and his cup of coffee. When they were seated in opposite aisle seats, the world of commerce resumed and a steady flow of paper went across to him for checkmarks, okays, and various other notations.

I am sure that inside I was grinning at him. For there had been a time when I was a would-be tycoon also, and thought that the world might possibly come to a screeching halt if I did not spend the hour or so in the air with an armload of something to read, write, check, or dictate. So it feels good now to check my bags, stroll on the plane in a sweater, slacks, and a pair of shoes that look like they belonged to a college professor, take the book from under my arm, and let the world run itself. In my mind I was smugly thinking, "I know what you are doing. I've done it myself and if you do it long enough and well enough maybe you can get to the place where you won't have to do it either." It was not one of my more compassionate moments.

In Chicago, ambling off in my writer-speaker gait to the Air Wisconsin departure lounge, I saw my traveling companion from 12C striding up the corridor full steam ahead with his secretary and the gear in tow. I sent him along with my hopes that he was able to buy the Loop or sell it or whatever.

In due time Air Wisconsin delivered me to Fort Wayne and I was taken to the downtown Holiday Inn for a weekend layman's retreat. It was not exactly my idea of "woodsy," but this was to be the place.

Having arrived early in the afternoon I decided to walk around the city some. Nearby, although the neighborhood had obviously gone through many changes and was even now in the process of urban renewal, there were some lovely old churches remaining. A sign on the front of one of them interested me. In my opinion, you can gain some insight both into the pastor and the congregation by the words and nuances of church signs. This was a new one to me. At first glance I thought it was some sort of a travesty. Walking along in the heart of the city dotted here and there with the poor and the down and the out, I wondered what I would have put on the sign in front of the church had I been the pastor. I don't think it would have been "Let the Good Times Roll."

Reluctant Belief in Last Things

Probably it was because after a smooth flight, a good lunch, and being checked into the complimentary Van Gogh Suite on the Concierge Floor, I wasn't as responsive as I might have been to the eschatological hope of the Christian.

I can remember when I was growing up that the word "hope" had great meaning to our congregation. They were a group of people with modest means. Many of them were factory workers making shoes in the first plant of Genesco, which was only a block away from the church on Main Street. Since they were not so deeply entrenched in the so-called good life we sang a lot of songs about our hopes in Jesus. Present circumstances were somehow tolerable, even with their attendant cares and sorrows, because they were viewed as only some kind of a temporary prelude to the real life we were someday going to live in his presence.

The great American dream slowly worked miracles in our midst. A generation or two later, we are all engrossed in somehow trying to make the present permanent, thinking that with time and a little luck we can take care of our own good times.

I am afraid I have the "this is the place" fever as bad as anyone. I walk around my house and acre and think of all the things I would like to do to them next. I want to extend the garden over here, move the driveway over there, build a picket fence, add a sun porch, and finish the attic. Meanwhile I'm planting perennials in the flower beds. But Jesus told us that he was going away to prepare us a place—a true, real place where we would finally really be at home. And when that place was ready—our authentic, "last-forever" place—he would come back and get us and take us there.

On two separate occasions recently I used the Lord's Supper as the background for the services in a retreat setting. We partook of the meal at the end of each meeting. Each time we varied the way we took the bread and the wine to try to let a different facet of their beauty and meaning shine through and become apparent to us.

One evening, in an attempt to better sense the oneness which the Lord's Table wants to bring to us, we stood in circles and spoke Christ's words to each other as we passed the loaf and the cup. In another service we held individual cups and pieces of bread and prayed solitary prayers that we might be made faithful to his plaintive plea to always remember him. One night we closed kneeling two by two all over the room, facing each other across altars made of chairs. Each partner took turns, as a communicant seeking the life of God, and as a priest affirming the presence of that life to the other by the laying on of our hands.

To close the weekend, we sat in quietness and prayer and awe at what these two sacramental things represent. One by one we came forward to take the elements. Both personally and publicly we wanted to join Christ in the dying that alone can lead to redemptive living.

There was one other thing that seemed to want to be said from this sacramental meal. It is the expression of Christian hope. Paul writes that we are to "proclaim the Lord's death *until he comes.*" In the Gospel versions, Jesus says that when this meal is eaten together again it will be in his Father's kingdom. It is the foundation of the great eschatological hope of the Christian. It is his promise that "the good times will roll."

In all honesty, this aspect of the communion was the hardest to define and the most difficult one to which to relate. It seemed to have the least appeal and inspiration to us all. Maybe it is because eschatology is the study of last things, and our first difficulty was that none of us wanted to think about end times or last things.

My dad has always been a stickler for detail and thorough planning. He has guided his life and fortunes with well thought-out plans and with copious notes of Plans A, B, and C written out in longhand, double-spaced on lined pads with carbon copies for everybody involved. Recently, he turned his penchant for planning to the final details of his life including his death, his funeral service and his burial. Needless to say, it was disconcerting to all of the family. Partly, I'm sure, it is because we do not want to think in terms of his dying. And partly it is because we know if we begin to think about his dying we will be reminded that everybody dies and that sooner or later the funeral and burial plans will be ours. So we had rather not think about endings at all.

For whatever the reason, whether it is preoccupation with the present, a reluctance to think about the future, or both, this great claim of the gospel has lost most of its appeal to us. As long as most of us have reasonably good health and prospects it is not a provision over which we are inclined to spend much time rejoicing.

The Promise of a Celebration

My dad is in his eighties now and has been in failing health for a long siege of months. In one of his plans, I don't know if it was A, B, or C, he wanted to sell his present home and acreage and see that my mother was comfortably fixed in a house and yard that was manageable for her. For, although she, too, is in her eighties, she works in the flower gardens and in the yard and keeps her house with remarkable zest and energy.

My brother John helped them find a place that was just right for the two of them. It had to be one with enough yard so that my mother would have room to plant some of her flowers, including some peonies that had passed along through her family for generations. The old place was sold and in preparation for the newer, smaller home, my mother began to give to her children and grandchildren pieces of furniture and silver that had been in her house as far back as I can remember. Among other things, she gave me the set of dessert forks that were a part of her silver from their wedding day. Out of all the things that I remember eating with them, her angel food cake with caramel sauce and whipped cream deliciously stands out the most in my memory.

The moving day came and the plan was first to move everything except Dad and his hospital bed and his big chair. He would then sit in the chair until they moved his bed and then they would take him down to the new place where his room would be all set up. My son Tom went by the old house just as all this was happening. The house was virtually empty, except for the nurse standing by and my dad sitting in his chair looking out the window at the Tennessee hills behind his place. Quietly, he was waiting for them to come to take him to his new home.

If you visit with him he will tell you, in a voice that is thin and weak and wracked with pain, that there is another move to another place that he is ready to make. And there he will be home forever.

I have been a reader and a lover of books for a long time. And I love the Bible because it closes like a book ought to close.

As a boy
I sailed the high seas,
        braved raging storms,
hacked through jungles,
        explored dark caves,
in hot pursuit of—
    "The Hardy Boys"
    "Tom Sawyer"
    "Robinson Crusoe"
    "Nancy Drew"
and other assorted heroes.
        They always
caught the villain,
        rescued the baby,
            won the battle,
found the money and
lived happily ever afterwards.

As I grew older
I began to read books in which
        the hero died
or the wrong guy married
        the fair young princess.
        You know the kind—
books with true-to-life endings.
    I guess I'm sentimental,
            probably even childish,
but I like books that end well.
    Let the hero be
    down and nearly out,
        shot and left for dead—
but let him win in the end.

And so I like the Bible—
        because it ends well.
it begins with the heros
        in a sinless, deathless land—
    but they tripped, fell,
        and got lost on a
a downward journey that led through
        sin, misery, failure,
            sorrow, war and shame.

And finally you begin to think
they are never going to
make it back.
But when it ends,
they are home again—
in a sinless, deathless land.
It took God's Son to do it—
but it ends well.

In these days with the world
divided into two camps—
glaring back and forth
like two little boys
across a line in the dust,
with hatred, strife,
wars and rumors—
with pain and death,
it helps me to know that
the One who started it well
will also see that it ends
according to His plan.[2]

The Bible does not deny the reality of suffering and evil. Neither of them are excluded from its pages in either the stories of the heros and heroines or in the stories of those who seem to be only tragic victims. But in the face of all the mishaps and misfortunes that have come along to befall the human race, the Bible continues to affirm that he will get us home. And when we get home there will be a celebration. In Matthew 22 Jesus describes the calling voice of God as an invitation to a banquet as joyous as a wedding feast.

Some summers ago, I was asked to perform a wedding for one of my cousins and his bride-to-be. It was to be a simple wedding in the home of the groom's mother with a feast to follow for all the guests. Sometimes, at marriages held in churches, the groom is so scared, and the bride is so worried about the dresses and the mothers are so sad that the whole affair has a kind of a somber tone. It doesn't help much either when the usher asks whose side you want to sit on, as if this was some sort of a contest instead of a celebration.

The Saturday of the wedding dawned and it was a perfectly gorgeous summer day. The afternoon could not have been prettier, the home was lovely and beautifully decorated. The couple-to-be stood in the entry hall laughing and greeting the guests. We were all friends and kinfolk, who don't get to see each other as much as we would like, and on this warm, sunny, summer afternoon, dressed in our Sunday best, we embraced each other and could hardly contain our joy. When everyone had arrived, I waited in front of the mantle in the living room as Ed and Jamie stood before me. Then all the guests, friends and loved ones gathered in a half circle around them to be truly a part of the ceremony.

I reminded this couple that people can fall in love and do. And, unfortunately, they can fall out of love too and tragically, sometimes do. But, I also told them, marriage is a miracle that only God can perform and together we prayed that he would truly perform his miracle on this waiting couple. They said their vows and presented rings and stood now with their right hands joined. The pronouncement was made and there were prayer and tears and rejoicing. I asked the groom if he would like to kiss his bride and he indicated that he would. And he did.

They turned, man and wife now, and the house was filled with congratulations and joy and hugs and kisses for everyone. There was also all about us the aroma of the feast and the sweet savor of hope and peace. It was like a phrase I had read somewhere and long ago appropriated for my wedding ceremonies, ". . . there were more smiles than faces and more happiness than hearts could contain."

In the parable of the wedding feast, Jesus is telling us that the calling of God is an invitation to a celebration. And the prospect of that celebration is the basis of the great hope the gospel proffers us all. Brennan Manning, a Catholic priest whose work is a ministry of solitude and retreat, wrote in his book, *Souvenirs of Solitude*, "Closely related to the quality of my faith is the intensity of my hope."[3] It is probably true for us all that faith and hope are so intertwined that the erosion of our need for hope in the gospel has also made its mark upon the reality of our faith. Like the invited guests of the parable, one going to the field and another to his business, we are so preoccupied with our own affairs that we do not have the time or the inclination to remember. But we are going to a celebration. The Bible ends with a feast. "The good times will roll."

A Faithful Father Waits

In the last two chapters of 1 Thessalonians Paul is writing about the second coming of Christ. In the fourth chapter, he assures the church there that "the Lord himself will come . . . and the dead in Christ will rise. After that, we who are still alive . . . will be caught up with them . . . to meet the Lord. And so we will be with the Lord forever. Therefore encourage each other with these words." I think he is telling us that the great foundation of our lives is to be found in the hope that these words alone can bring.

In the benediction of 1 Thessalonians 5 Paul writes that the certainty of this hope is to be found in the faithfulness of God: "The one who calls you is faithful and he will do it."

The calling of God comes to us in the ways that I have been writing about. It can be heard deep within and it can be heard in the community of believers. It speaks to us from the providences and the purposes of God. It makes demands on us for commitments and for consecrations. It summons us to holiness and purity even as it warns us to flee evil and wickedness. To truly answer it requires of us the dedication of all of the best that we are or can be. Paul tells us, though, that the steadfastness of our hope does not rest on the strength of our arm, nor in the doggedness of our determination. Our hope rests securely in the everlasting faithfulness and goodness of the One who has called us. He is faithful and he will get us home.

For a long time when it was halftime at football games, I wished the bands would finish and get off the field so we could get back to watching the real action. A time came, however, when I could hardly wait for the half to be over so the field would be cleared of ball players and referees. Now the main event could begin! Patrick had joined the band.

When our youngest son joined the high school band, he introduced us to a world we had not even known existed as we followed our other four through this period of their lives. We learned that "band-itry," like most everything else Americans do, was a subculture all its own. It has its own rules, regulations, contests, performances, championships, trophies, winners, losers, pageantry, intricate marching patterns, and exciting music.

At Patrick's school, the Marching Cougars began their season the first week in August with a six-day camp of rigorous drill and rehearsal to learn the show for the coming season. The director had already spent the first two months of the summer working on the musical arrangements and the drill itself. We always looked forward to the last day of camp, for there was an exciting (although ragged) first performance for the parents.

Every weekday afternoon for the rest of August, the band was on the practice field polishing the music and marching steps. Early in September, the performances would begin at the Friday night football games both at home and away. There were also contests and band festivals on Saturdays which were all a part of the process leading up to the third Saturday in October when the Class A State Championship was held.

The climactic afternoon and evening of the state championship was a colorful panorama of bands, parents, hot dogs, music, buses, nachos, an occasional dog on the field, and the all-time All-American pastime, competition. Beginning promptly at 1:00 P.M. and every twelfth minute thereafter, there was a band of trained, excited, nervous, talented kids lined up on the far side of the field awaiting the voice of the announcer over the loudspeaker: "Field Commander, is your band ready?" This inquiry was answered by the major or majorettes in an unbelievable set of motions, gyrations and leaps that transformed the tipping of the hat and the nodding of the head into a ten-second extravaganza in itself. The announcer, over the roar of the crowd, a roar most often led by the majorette's mother and father, acknowledged this magnificent salute to readiness with the words that have been anticipated since the first moments of rehearsal camp, "You may begin!"

In the next eight minutes (playing too long lowers the score) all of the hours of rehearsal and drill are put on the line. Late in the afternoon, the six finalists are announced and after a break for supper and for the spectators to get warm, the stands fill up again and the final competition begins for the trophies—First Place and the Governor's Cup. Each of the six bands repeats its performances but this time with the excitement and confidence of being in the finals and with the hope now of being number one. The good directors, like Mr. Van Dyke, had saved a wrinkle or two for the finals. The faces in the percussion section were painted, one side blue and one side white.

When the bands have finished and the judges are finally ready to make their decisions known, the six bands are standing in a row in formation on the field. And the loudspeakers blare forth, "The number six band with a score of 84.5 is. . . . the number five band is. . . . number four. . . . three. . . ." And a great roar goes up when the name of the number two band is sounded forth. A tremendous roar that drowns out the cheers for Number Two because the only band left unnamed, and its rooting section of parents and friends, has suddenly realized that there is nobody else left between them and the championship. They are Number One!

It is a moment of almost unbearable pride and excitement if your kid is one of the members of the band they are naming when they say, "And the number one band in the state with a score of 94.5 is. . . ." Three years in a row, Patrick and the Marching Cougars were the band in which this delirious bedlam broke out. There was another year when some three-quarters of a point taught them the agonies of defeat.

The high point of a band's performance is the closer, or push, as Patrick's director called it. Usually it begins with the band close to the stands playing their final song. The intricate patterns have been marched and the percussion break has been played—and the band is in tight formation. There is a section of the music that is played softly and the band marches away, backs to the crowd. Then they wheel and march toward the stands playing full volume for the finale. It is called "blowing to the box" because the band gives the judges everything they have.

I asked Patrick if he could describe what it was like marching toward the stands filled with cheering parents and friends, playing wide open with all that paint on his face and finally coming to attention as the last echoes of the music of the concluding song of the final show are lost in the noise of the crowd. He grinned as if it were impossible to explain. I told him that if he thought it was exciting on the field he should just wait until a day somewhere, sometime when he was a dad at a state championship. And then he would see his kid turn and march toward him in perfect step with a hundred other kids, his head high and his back straight, beating fifty pounds of drums as if it were his task to set the tempo for the whole world. I told him if I was still around, I wanted to be sitting there with him. And then we can talk about what thrilling *really* is.

My thinking about this nudged me into some further thoughts about the heavenly Father. This One who is calling us. We all tend to believe (or at least fear) that the God who calls us is watching us. It makes all the difference in the world where we think he is sitting. As long as we think of him as the judge in the pressbox who is checking for smudges on our white shoes, for the misplayed notes, for marching out of step, for our hats falling off or any one of a dozen other things that can happen to us in our performance, it is hard to keep from living our whole lives in fear of a button coming off our tunics. It was Jesus himself who reminded us that we were to call him Father— "Abba Father"—which is a lot more like calling him Dad. I think Jesus was telling us that our Father is the one in the stands who is standing on the seat, waving his coat in a circle over his head with tears of pride and happiness running down his face.

"He is the one who called us and he is faithful." He will get us home.

See you at the house.

End Notes

Chapter 1

1. Thomas Merton, "Rain and the Rhinoceros," from *Raids on the Unspeakable* (New York: New Directions, 1966) p. 10.
2. Norman Cousins, *The Healing Heart* (New York: W. W. Norton and Company, 1983) p. 141-142.
3. Willa Cather, *Death Comes for the Archbishop* (New York: Random House, 1927, 1955) p. 50.
4. Robert Frost, quoted in *Robert Frost, a Tribute to the Source* (New York: Holt, Rinehart and Winston, 1979) p. 105.

Chapter 2

1. Albert Edward Day, *Dialogue and Destiny* (New York: Harper and Row, 1961) p. 89.
2. Rainer Maria Rilke, *Letters to a Young Poet*, translated by M. D. Herter Norton (New York: W. W. Norton and Company, 1934) p. 19-20.
3. Elizabeth-Paul Labat, *The Presence of God* (New York: Paulist Press, 1979) p. 46.
4. Evelyn Underhill, *The Spiritual Life* (Wilton: Morehouse-Barlow Company, 1937, 1938, 1955) p. 20.
5. Annie Dillard, *Teaching a Stone to Talk* (New York: Harper and Row, 1982) p. 15-16.

6. Thomas Merton, *Life and Holiness* (New York: Doubleday and Company, 1963) p. 12.
7. Kahil Gibran, *The Prophet* (New York: Alfred A. Knopf, r 1951) p. 17–18.
8. M. Basil Pennington, *Centering Prayer* (New York: Doubleday and Company, 1980) p. 102.

Chapter 3

1. Cardinal Suhard, quoted in the introduction to *By Little and By Little: The Selected Writings of Dorothy Day*, Robert Ellsberg ed. (New York: Alfred A. Knopf, 1983) p. xv.
2. Evelyn Underhill, *Abba* (Wilton: Morehouse-Barlow Company, 1981) p. 21.
3. Renata Adler, quoted in *People, Books and Book People*, by David McCollough (New York: Harmony Books, 1980, 1981) p. 1.
4. Clarence Day, quoted in *Quotations of Wit and Wisdom*, ed. John W. Gardner and Francesca Gardner Reese (New York: W. W. Norton and Company, 1975) p. 97.
5. Stuart Briscoe, *Romans, The Communicator's Commentary*, ed. Lloyd Ogilvie (Waco: Word Books, Publisher, 1982) p. 176.
6. Roger Von Oech, *A Whack on the Side of the Head: How to Unlock Your Mind for Innovation*, (New York: Warner Books, 1983) p. 64.
7. Jess Lair, *Ain't I a Wonder and Ain't You a Wonder Too?* (New York: Doubleday and Company, 1977) p. 53–54.
8. Ibid, p. 54.
9. Evelyn Underhill, p. 9.
10. Will Campbell, *God on Earth* (New York: Crossroads Publishing Company, 1983) p. 20.

Chapter 4

1. M. L. Haskins. I have heard this quote many times over the years. Recently it came into my life again on a plaque that was given to me.
2. I am indebted for the idea of this discussion of asthma to an interesting description of the effects it had on Teddy Roosevelt. It was a part of David McCullough's book, *Mornings on Horseback*. See Chapter Four.
3. Dorothee Soelle, *Death by Bread Alone* (Philadelphia: Fortress Press, 1978) p. 32–33.
4. Phil Johnson and Bob Benson, *Give Them All* (Nashville: Dimension Music, The Benson Company, 1975). © Copyright 1975 by The Benson Company. All rights reserved. Used by permission.

Chapter 5

1. Abraham Joshua Heschel, *Man's Quest for God* (New York: Charles Scribner's Sons, 1954) p. 5.
2. Truman Capote, *A Christmas Memory* (New York: Random House, 1956) p. 42–43.

3. Erma Bombeck, "One of These Days," Field Enterprises Inc.
4. Frederick Buechner, *Wishful Thinking* (New York: Harper and Row, 1973) p. 82–83.
5. Harold E. Fey, *The Lord's Supper* (New York: Harper and Row, 1948).
6. Hans Küng, *The Church* (New York: Doubleday and Company, 1967) p. 291.
7. Thomas G. Pettepiece, *Visions of a World Hungry* (Nashville: Upper Room, 1979).

Chapter 6

1. Emilie Griffin, *Clinging* (New York: Harper and Row, 1984) p. 5–6.
2. Catherine de hueck Doherty, *Poustinia, Christian Spirituality of the East for Western Man* (Notre Dame: Ave Maria Press, 1975) p. 27.
3. Ibid, p. 21–22.
4. Henri J. M. Nouwen, *Making All Things New: An Invitation to the Spiritual Life* (New York: Harper and Row, 1981) p. 21.
5. Annie Dillard, *Teaching a Stone to Talk* (New York: Harper and Row, 1982) p. 31.

Chapter 7

1. Anthony Bloom, *Beginning to Pray* (New York: Paulist Press, 1970) p. 41–42.
2. Martin Marty, *A Cry of Absence* (New York: Harper and Row, 1983) p. 33.
3. James Finley, *Merton's Place of Nowhere* (Notre Dame: Ave Maria Press, 1978).
4. Jim Russell, "Seems to Me," *The American Way.*
5. Abraham Joshua Heschel, *Man Is Not Alone: A Philosophy of Religion* (New York: Farrar, Straus and Giroux, 1951) p. 180–182.
6. Bob Benson, *Meanings*, Volume 3, Number 9, p. 4.

Chapter 8

1. Jane Howard, *Families* (New York: Simon and Schuster, 1978) p. 29
2. Abraham Joshua Heschel, *Man's Quest for God* (New York: Charles Scribner's Sons, 1954) p. 80.
3. Abraham Joshua Heschel, *God in Search of Man* (New York: Farrar, Straus and Giroux, 1955, 1983).
4. Leo Buscaglia, *Living, Loving, Learning* (Thorofare: Charles B. Slack, Inc., 1982) p. 93.
5. Virginia Stem Owens, *And the Trees Clap Their Hands* (Grand Rapids: William B. Eerdmans Publishing Company, 1983) p. 147.
6. Lewis Thomas, *The Youngest Science: Notes of a Medicine Watcher* (New York: Viking Press, 1983).
7. Henri J. M. Nouwen, *Gracias* (New York: Harper and Row, 1983) p. 16.
8. I had read of this experiment before, but I could not help but be influenced by Leo Buscaglia's account in *Living, Loving, Learning*, p. 36–37.
9. Jane Howard, *Families* (New York: Simon and Schuster, 1978) p. 269–270.

10. Ralph Keyes, We. the Lonely People (New York: Harper and Row, 1973) p. 216.
11. Kurt Kaiser, O How He Loves You and Me. © Copyright 1975 by Word Music (A Div. of Word, Inc.). All rights reserved. International Copyright Secured. Used by Permission.

Chapter 9

1. Aleksandr I. Solzhenitsyn, The Oak and the Calf (New York: Harper and Row, 1975) p. 3.
2. Irvin S. Cobb quoted in Quotations of Wit and Wisdom, ed. John W. Gardner and Francesca Gardner Reese (New York: W. W. Norton and Company, 1975) p. 164.
3. Andrew Greeley, Thy Brother's Wife (New York: Warner Books, 1982) p. 305.
4. Mary Strong, ed. Letters to the Scattered Brotherhood (New York: Harper and Row, 1948) p. 7–8.
5. Dag Hammarskjöld, Markings (New York: Alfred A. Knopf, Inc., 1964) p. 74.
6. C. S. Lewis, Mere Christianity (New York: Macmillan Publishing Company, 1952) p. 86.
7. Abraham Joshua Heschel, Man is Not Alone: A Philosophy of Religion (New York: Farrar, Straus and Giroux, 1951) p. 88.

Chapter 10

1. Leo Buscaglia, Living, Loving, Learning (Thorofare: Charles B. Slack, Inc., 1982) p. 195.
2. Bob Benson, Laughter in the Walls (Brentwood: Solitude and Celebration Press, 1969) p. 66–67.
3. Brennan Manning, Souvenirs of Solitude (Denville: Dimension Books, 1979) p. 15.